About the author

Chuck Spezzano, Ph.D.
counsellor, trainer, author, lecturer and visionary
leader. He holds a Doctorate in Psychology. From 30
years of counselling experience and 26 years of
psychological research and seminar leadership, Dr
Spezzano and his wife, Lency, created the
breakthrough therapeutic healing model Psychology of
Vision. The impact of this model has brought deep
spiritual, emotional and material change to thousands
of participants from around the world.

50 Ways to Let Go and Be Happy

CHUCK SPEZZANO, Ph.D.

CORONET BOOKS

Hodder & Stoughton

The right of Chuck Spezzano to be identified as the Author of the Work
has been asserted by him in accordance with the Copyright, Designs
and Patents Act 1988.

First published in Great Britain in 2001 by Hodder and Stoughton
A division of Hodder Headline

A Coronet Paperback

10 9 8 7 6 5 4 3

A CIP catalogue record for this title is available from the British Library.

ISBN 0 340 79352 X

Typeset by Palimpsest Book Production Limited,
Polmont, Stirlingshire
Printed and bound in Great Britain by
Mackays of Chatham plc, Chatham, Kent

Hodder and Stoughton
A division of Hodder Headline
338 Euston Road
London NW1 3BH

To my sister, Kathy, and brother-in-law Bill
for the angels you are.

Acknowledgements

First of all, I would like to acknowledge the brilliant editing that brought this book to its present state. Thank you Sue Allen, Karen Sullivan and Brian Mayne. For typing and general support, I want to acknowledge Peggy Chang and Kathy Miller-Strobel. Thank you to my students who have taught me so well. I would like to acknowledge my wife, Lency, and my children, Christopher and J'aime, for their love, support and the grace they are to me. Thank you all for the wondrous and helpful part you play in my life.

I would also like to acknowledge *A Course in Miracles* for the extent to which it has influenced my life in an ongoing way, giving me an ever-deepening understanding of psychology and spirituality. It has shown me a path home.

Contents

Preface

I have lost count of how many times I have thought, 'I wish I had known this when I was younger.' Through individual, relationship, and workshop counselling sessions over the years, I have learned many healing principles. When I, or others, suffered, I focused on the heart of the problem to find what was causing it and how to get out of it. I learned most of these principles as I suffered through problems myself, and discovered what worked. Then I used them in my therapeutic practice and found they had universal application. What I learned made all the difference in helping people to heal themselves quickly. These principles have been tried and tested by years of counselling, and have been found to transcend culture. I have used them freely and effectively in Asia, North America and Europe.

I only wish I had known these principles when I began my own relationships. It would have saved me a lot of time, trouble and heartache. For many years, I have told stories about *Baca Sensei*. In Japanese *Baca* means stupid or foolish and *Sensei* means teacher. *Baca Sensei* was the one who had to make all of the mistakes himself, so he could teach the lessons he had learned. I am that one. It's amazing how people can laugh and enjoy the stories of experiences that were pure horror for me when they occurred.

I have found the principle of 'letting go' to be one of the most crucial principles in life and relationships. It has not been an easy lesson for me. I went to the Olympics in 'holding on'. I found that my Mediterranean background naturally confused boundaries and made a habit of 'fusion' (see page 194), which always intensifies any problem.

Having learned these important lessons, I now share them with you. Given a little application, you will find these principles work, whether you believe them or not.

This book is about happiness and how to achieve it. It is about what stands in the way of happiness – in particular, the 'holding-on' of old relationships. As I travelled in North America, Asia and Europe, I found that one of the most frequent problems presented to me involved the emotional pain and debris left over from old relationships. The problem most frequently presented was not having a partner; in close second, then, were the problems associated with letting go of old relationships. It was clear that there was a link between these issues.

This book concentrates on what is ultimately the most important element in our lives – happiness. By learning how to let go of the attachments and other aspects of old relationships that secretly or not so secretly keep us from living life in the present, we will become open to a new or deeper love relationship now.

We're at a dramatic time in the development of our society. Many are finding that we have the trappings of success without any enjoyment. We have many things we thought would make us happy and yet we aren't happy. This is an important crossroads, for it forces us to confront issues: either we strive harder, give up and change goals, or we learn about ourselves, relationships and the inner experience and expression of life. Today, people work harder and harder just to stay in the same place – which has obvious ramifications on overall happiness, motivation and our perception of the world around us. Yet, at some point in our development we will learn that it is the further expression of our hearts, minds and spirits that makes us happy rather than an accumulation of 'things', our level of career success and our bottom line. These are all good things, but in a hundred years' time, they will be largely irrelevant.

Working with pensioners has led me to the understanding that life is about so much more than material achievement. These men and women have made clear the fact that their regrets surround not what they did in their lives, but what they didn't do. And it's in the area of relationships and family that this regret is most commonly expressed. Holding on to the past is the best way to jeopardise present happiness, particularly holding on in relationships and family.

When we are attached to the past – and any pain is a ultimately a sign that we are holding onto past pain – every pain expresses a pattern of unfinished emotional business and unmet needs from the past. Letting go is one of the easiest of healing principles, if and when we have the courage to do it. The courage and trust to let go allows a rebirth in our lives and the chance for present happiness. It's time we learned to understand this process, in order to succeed in that all-important area of happiness in relationships.

Research shows there are typically a number of emotional crises in each person's life that are serious enough to result in hospitalisation. Suffering a loss can be one of the main causes of this. Although this book is written specifically about the loss of a relationship, it can easily be used in other significant situations, including the death of a loved one, the end of a job, or the loss of material possessions. At these times, when it would be so important to have a therapist, counsellor, coach or wise friend to talk to, many people do not have access to these or cannot afford the help. This book is meant to be that wise friend for those who need it, to assist those who really want, but cannot find or afford, professional help, and to come to the aid of those who are solitary in their pain and who just want to do it for themselves.

Although the problems that arise from not letting go can last a lifetime, my experience is that finding the solution can occur very quickly, sometimes in just an hour or two. Half a dozen years ago, I was shocked when someone told me of an excellent therapist and author who had cited two to three years as being the 'normal' time required to heal a given problem. I could not imagine any problem taking this long to heal. Some problems may last that long or even longer, but working through the subconscious can greatly accelerate the process.

With willingness and the right circumstances, a problem can be healed in an hour or two. I have seen chronic or major problems, such as cancer, alcoholism, an inability to express emotion, screaming nightmares, borderline psychosis or even allergies, clear up in an hour. While this book is designed as a 50-way process, any healing can actually be completed by doing any one of the lessons. You simply need to do it so well that the rest of the lessons (while still helpful) will actually be superfluous to your particular healing process. If this occurs, I still recommend that you go through the rest of the lessons for your own education. They will round and smooth out the healing process, and help in healing whatever other problems you might have now or meet in the future.

This book, while not religious, has spiritual principles within it. Over the years I have found that only a fine line can be drawn between higher psychological and spiritual principles. Hopefully, this book is general enough for these principles to fit into your own religious or spiritual framework. Such a framework can be of great assistance in accelerating your healing process.

Like an old friend, this book is meant to be more than just a one-time experience. You can go back to it time and again, and learn and heal more each time you do. It contains over 30 years' worth of learning and wisdom, and it's written in 'layers', so there is something for everyone, from beginners to veteran therapists. Each time you come back to it, new understandings will emerge.

Life is bigger than any theory. Principles that come from first-hand experience over many years are only as good as the artist/author/scientist who attempts to describe them. This book is not meant to contain all there is to know about letting go. It represents a way through whatever challenge you are facing. May it be a step to opening up a new and better present and future for you. May it show you the way to be happy and joyous in true love once more.

Chuck Spezzano
Hawaii 2001

I Am Happiness

I Am Happiness.

If you chase me, you'll never catch me.
  If you want me above all else, I am yours.
If you look for me in form, I shall disappoint you.
  If you find me in form, I shall leave while you are
    asleep.

If you be a true seeker, then reach beyond your self.

Where peace and innocence abide, there shall I pitch
  my tent.
  Love is the only cup from which I drink.
You cannot take me – I can only be received.
  You cannot buy me – I can only be given.

Only when you forget me can I come.

I'm never solo, always shared.
  I join the hands that trust.
When armed with truth, there are no casualties in my
  name.
  I take no prisoners.

Choose me.

You cannot be right and happy, too.

No victim knows me.
Have you not sold me for 30 pieces of pain,
  because I am gone when you are withdrawn and
    wounded?

Being right is only an attempt to cover how wrong
  you feel.

When you feel wrong you punish yourself and others.
  Every victim gets to be right – sometimes dead right,
    always dead-end.
Victims and victimisers are opposite sides of the same
  coin,
  looking for love in all the wrong places.

I am crucified by sacrifice, but I am the perennial
  promise of resurrection.

If death can stop you, you think I'm outside you.
  If you could be content with only your small self,
you know the true meaning of ghetto –
  and what shall I do with this deed to the universe?

Choose me.

It's never a question of ability; it's always a question of
  willingness.
  Lemming-like, you choose death; I am the Gate of Life.
Surrender, I've got you surrounded.
  You're outnumbered.

I am One – you are five billion.

If you want me weak, look without you.
  If you want me strong, look within.
Why do you choose a time that always runs out on you?
  I am with you now.

Choose me.

Compare and I get lost in the shuffle of forms.
  Compete and you believe in loss;
their loss is your future pain.
  What you believe you see.

Winning and losing promotes a belief in scarcity.
  I come not out of your abundance, but it comes out
    of Me.
If you stand for something, you'll be a character witness.
  That's only one of the courtroom roles you will play.

Judge, jury, prosecution, defence.

I am not there.
  If Happiness does not stand for it, why should you?
Nobody makes me.
  You cannot create me.

I always AM.

But in your creation you claim me.
  I'm never doing, I'm always Being.
If you can't find me, look with forgiving eyes.
  Whatever it is you want, give it, so you can have it
    as yours.

Choose me.

If you are tempted, you think I'm in form.
　If you are tempted, you think I'm outside you.
If you are tempted, you are just doing time.
　Only what tempts you can kill you.
Your temptation is just another way to hide old pain.

Feel temptation:
　it glitters, but it isn't gold.
Feel Happiness:
　how long can you let me love you and not turn away?

Choose me.

I am here, now, within, loving you.
　Where are you running off to again?
All of your seeking will only find Me where you began.
　How long must I wait?

That you are a creature of habit makes you a creature.

Another quest to go on, another question.
　Will you ever get closer to here and now?
The words, 'It's only a matter of time,'
　can either be the last hope or the death sentence.

What is it in YOUR life?

It's never a question of time, it's always a question
　of nerve.
　If you have the time, I have the nerve.

When you go off in pursuit,
  you can be depressed before or after you succeed,

for different reasons.

If you're depressed,
  what loss have you not let go of?
Are judgements and mourning better than Happiness
  now?
  I'm here, now, waiting.

Choose Me.

From Desire to disillusionment there is but a short
  space.
  When disillusionment comes you think life is hard and
  you die.
Do not look for Me where I cannot be found.
  Search for Me in a thousand, thousand things –

I am not there.

Can you bear the disappointment?
  Will you promise not to die of a broken heart?
Will you swear that I deserted you when I have never left
  you here alone;
    but another crusade is coming for you to curse me in
      your leaving.

Choose me.

You are to learn I am no-thing but All-things.
  What identity would keep you from me?

Only desperadoes need disguises.
   Turn yourself in – collect your reward.

Choose me.

The acid test of happiness is this, if it can get past
   the words:
   'You can't take it with you.'
Only that which you can hold onto in the face of death,
   and have death disappear, adds to your happiness.

If you are not happy, what is more important to you
   than me?

You can still choose.

Choose me now, for I am the gift that Heaven has
   given you.
   Choose me now, for I am the gift of life itself.
Choose me now, for I am your birthright.
   Choose me now, for I am the gift of love giving to love.

Choose me now, for I am the remembrance of who you
   really are.

It is so simple.
   In spite of everything,

Choose me Now.

I Am Happiness.

WAY 1 Happiness is the Best Revenge

Happiness is what life is all about. It is heaven on earth, if only for a moment. Happiness is the element of our lives on which it is most important to concentrate. Any other focus is something that our ego has engineered to make itself stronger, selling us a bill of goods that it promises will bring us happiness. When it falls well short, we are left in vicious circles of pain, indulgence and scarcity (see page 195), which increases our separation from truth and love.

As we grow, we build up our ego to get along in the world. As we evolve towards partnership, we begin to move the barriers of the ego. The ego tries to teach us that specialness, which is the desire to be treated as the most special one and have others dedicated to meeting our needs, is love, and that winning over others is more important than winning together. The ego hides fear and espouses guilt, neither of which is remotely helpful. The ego plans campaigns of suffering and heartbreak, establishes our role as a victim or victimiser and, finally, when we are disappointed and disillusioned enough by false goals, it plans our death. If we measure this against the experience of happiness, it is crazy to follow the path of the ego. It has a million traps, dark stories, conspiracies, false gods and shadow figures, all of which are a means of deceiving us to follow the path of revenge and rebellion, rather than the path of life.

Let me introduce the idea of revenge. Do not be floored by it. Revenge is one of the most hidden of any dynamics to any problem. This is not a concept that you must fully grasp now, but it is something that you will need eventually to understand, and of which you will need to become aware. The fact that we are not happy is evidence that revenge has taken over our lives. Gradually, as we learn about revenge and catch ourselves from making that mistake, our life improves in many ways. So here are some of the main reasons we keep revenge going. Don't try to understand it all in one day. It is something most people spend a lifetime learning.

Revenge comes from a rejection or heartbreak that we set up to pay off guilt, to do things our way, to hide from our purpose, while pretending we are too small to fulfil our potential and what we promised at a soul level. Revenge is a dead end that is built on power struggles and pain. Revenge, which always stems from a revenge on our parents, is also a revenge on God, blaming Him for a world that we have created and circumstances that we have set up as an ego plan to get something. In this plot against our parents and God, we become the ultimate prodigal child, making bad choices, squandering our inheritance, enduring suffering and independence, all the time being too proud to ask for help. We have taken rebellion to new heights, projecting our feelings and mistakes on God and then disbelieving in Him if not by word then by action. This is not *just* a metaphor. It is the deepest expression of the traps of our minds. We will further examine this in the next to last Way (see page 181).

The question is not really how we could be so foolish as to make such bad investments, but why are we foolish enough to continue making them when happiness awaits us? There is a path to happiness that is both general to everyone and specific to us. Why aren't we more curious about this? Could happiness be so simple and true? This path of happiness could make all the difference in our lives, showing us the way out of the path of pain that our ego convinced us would make us happy through revenge. Why don't more of us want to find the way out of our traps? Instead of happiness, we continue to choose the weary road to death.

Happiness takes no hostages and carries no baggage. It lives in the here and now. It does not carry records or files on people, and allows them to be eternally themselves rather than relegated to past performance or a lack thereof. Happiness is not naïve, but aware. It does not deceive itself or others. It does not want to take but only to give, and is therefore able to receive and reap as happily as it sows. Happiness recognises only blessings from the past and in what is to come. Yet, happiness knows that it comes from a simple choice to receive with grace. Happiness is simple and uncomplicated. I wants to be shared to increase itself. It is a gift to everyone around us. It tells God, our parents, our lovers, spouses, friends and children that they have not failed us now or ever, in any way. Happiness is the part of the present that is like eternity. It is a gift from a loving God and a matter of choice. Happiness eschews judgement, knowing that it hides guilt, which sets up grievances and unhappy patterns, and locks us into the problem rather than providing solutions that would lead to innocence.

Happiness brings us back to our centres, and requires nothing other than the choice to be happy. There is nothing we need do for happiness because it is present within us. All that is necessary is letting go of what is in the way. Happiness is best friends with forgiveness; one always leads to the other. Happiness holds on to nothing, knowing that attachment blocks receiving at a higher level. Our attachment to how good or how bad things were prevents opportunities for happiness now. Happiness comes from a realisation of abundance, love and creativity that wants to be shared. It is simple and profound; open and clear; strong and tender. Happiness is a party that invites everyone, knowing that joy is increased by inclusion. Happiness blames not, and is therefore free from blame. Happiness receives all good things, and is always choosing to look on the bright side of life. On the path of happiness, we are led forward by signs of greater happiness.

Happiness knows that revenge is a dead end. In no way can revenge ever make us happy. When we embrace happiness, we embrace and know our destiny, and who we have come to be on earth. Similarly when we are happy, we treat ourselves as we treat others. Happiness gives up rebelliousness and listens to the truth.

Happiness wants to share itself with us if we would only listen.

Exercise

Examine your life, particularly the areas where you are not happy. These are the places where you are getting revenge on both everyone involved in the present situation and those from the past, including your parents and God. Because you think that people failed you, you believe that you can be independent and forever do it your way. Somehow you thought that running away rather than healing would make you happy. You thought that something other than choosing happiness, in this case revenge or rebellion, would make you happy in these situations.

Choose happiness once again now, today and every-day. You may have set up layers of complicated traps that have made you unhappy, but each choice takes you a layer closer to happiness. Embrace your happiness now and forever. Once realised, your happiness will want to share itself to help others feel the joy. In this way, i will continue to increase.

WAY 2 To Be Happy, Let Go

Let's face it, there are many reasons to be unhappy – enough reasons to last a lifetime. Yet the experience we have in life depends so much on our attitude and what we ultimately want and choose. Facing a loss is no different. In the final essay, we choose what will occur and how this will affect our lives. 'That which does not kill you, makes you stronger.' And, thus, we choose what any experience will mean to us.

Think about the loss you have suffered. What did you want to occur? What do you hope will be the final result of this loss? Do you want it to be the end of you, or the beginning of a whole new level? Do you want your life to stop here, or do you want to learn the lesson involved, and become more successful and loving? Do you want your pain to be a monument to the relationship and its ending? Or do you want to receive the love that was given and let happiness become a way of life for you? Will this be a problem that you will never get over, or will it be the springboard to a whole new level in relationships? Do you want to wear a long face the rest of your life, stating: 'I am this way, because this person has done this to me? It is at this one's hands that I have been broken?' This is your revenge: to remain emotionally wounded, to state whoever hurt you could not be a good person if they were willing to leave you so forlorn. Do you really want to hurt yourself to get revenge? Would not happiness be more effective in every way?

Exercise

Ask yourself what you are trying to prove by allowing the letting-go process to unfold the way it has. When you get your answer, ask yourself what you are proving by that. When you get your answer to this question, ask yourself what you are proving by it, and continue to ask and answer this question with each new answer that is revealed. You could do this for thirty to forty minutes, or until you get to a place of bliss. Each response reveals a compensation (see page 193). As you get to the next, deeper response, the previous layer falls away. This is a very simple way to get through and let go of many self-concepts. Trust what comes into your mind.

What you are trying to prove is simply the self-concept or identity that you are trying to support. It is a compensation – something you are trying to prove, but do not really believe. You could choose happiness instead of what you are trying to prove. Happiness already contains everything you could possibly want. It is important to realise that any specific letting-go or problem may have several, or even hundreds, of layers. Yet, each choice moves you through one or more layers and forward toward happiness.

WAY 3   The Story of Your Life

Human beings are story-telling creatures. At the deepest layers of the mind there is energy, and then the mind differentiates into symbols, archetypes, myths and stories. We give our lives meaning and, as such, we tell a certain story about them. And we are telling it for a certain purpose. Our story sets up the most primordial patterns of our lives, which are more fundamental than, and also generate, family patterns. Since the major traps in life, relationship and victim patterns, are generated through the family pattern, our story line has one of the most generative effects on our lives. It is a soul pattern.

Now reflect on how your loss fits into your story. Is it a minor point in your life story? Is it just a step in building towards ultimate success? Is it another tragedy in a long, tragic story? Is it the turning point in the story for better or for worse? What happens after this? Is it the climax or just the opening action? This last loss is a chapter in your story. What is the title of that chapter? What will the next chapter be called? How are you going to continue telling this story? You are able to choose all of this. What do you want in your life? Do you want a happy story, a love story, an adventure story or a discovery story?

The ultimate power we have is to choose and

to continue to choose a story that we really want. Choosing what we want leads us to it. Choices made continuously in a similar direction become an attitude.

Exercise

If your life was a movie, what would be the title? What would be the story of the movie? Who would you be getting revenge on by this movie?

Take a page and, writing in a 'stream of consciousness' manner, let the story of your movie come out as quickly as you can, or use a tape recorder and record it. Examine what's happened and is happening in your life and the story you have written or recorded as your movie. Where are they similar? Remembering that your story sets the pattern of your life and experience, consider how the pattern of your movie manifests itself in your life. What is your purpose for having this story or having this loss in your story? What story would you choose now?

WAY 4   Happiness Is the Goal

Happiness must be our goal if we are to avoid losing ourselves, and what is true, in the midst of our busy lives. Our perspective and priorities about what is true and important have been distorted, shattered and lost as a result of our fractured bonding while growing up. As a result, we live lives fuelled by adrenaline, rather than happiness. We get caught up in busyness, consumerism, deadness, withdrawal, sacrifice, indulgence, independence, dissociation and quiet desperation. We manufacture drama, or even violence, in an effort to feel something in our lives.

If we realise that happiness is the goal, and the best means to the goal, then we know we are heading in the right direction. If our goal is something other than happiness, if we are feeling something other than happiness, then we must change course to get ourselves back to the centre of our lives. Our centre is not a place of selfishness; it is a place of bonding and true perspective. We have deeper and deeper centres within us, all bringing us to a greater understanding and happiness. As a result of fractured bonding, we set up many mistaken goals that will not satisfy us. Without happiness, our lives become an ever smaller, vicious circle of indulgence, sacrifice to pay off the guilt of indulgence, then indulgence to attempt to relieve the burn-out of sacrifice, then sacrifice to pay off this guilt, and so on.

Happiness, love, giving-receiving, creativity, truth, balance, bonding, centredness and non-attachment are all similarly connected. As we head for happiness, we know that we are finally headed for the truth. All of us think that we *are* actually heading towards happiness in whatever it is that we do, but we have often made grave errors in our choices about what we thought would make us happy. If we have a problem or an unhappy situation, this is a sure sign that we made a mistake about what we thought would bring us happiness. And these decisions can be made in a split second, and then repressed so we may not remember making them.

With awareness, we can catch ourselves before we mistakenly choose pain, problems, illness, failure, revenge or loss. We can then choose truth and happiness. If we find ourselves in a problem or painful predicament, we can make the choice for happiness once again. We can admit that we were wrong in what we thought would make us happy and ask heaven to show us the way back to happiness.

Let us all be students in the school of happiness. As we learn what really makes us happy, we move forward from one step of evolution to the next. Happiness is the only valid measuring stick for our lives. If it is missing, then something is off centre. We have lost our balance and our perspective. Happiness does not live in the future or the past, but in the here and now. If our lives do not add up to happiness, then we must change if we want to be happy. As we continuously make the choice for happiness, we learn that we must keep letting go of our past, our attachments, our indulgence and other counterfeit forms of happiness. With happiness as our goal, we become more educated and wise as we follow its unfolding path. We can have more and more happiness in our lives now, and in all the future nows. As we go, we learn how to bring more happiness into our own lives, and those of other people.

Exercise

Today, assess your life for how much happiness is there in general, and in particular. How well are you doing? See areas of poor results as areas of mistaken choices about happiness. Commit to happiness. Ask to be shown the way. Take time at least once a week and repeat this exercise for the rest of your life. Commitment sets you on the proper road again even if only for a while. You may have many blocks between you and happiness in a certain area of your life, but every commitment brings you that much closer.

The Nature of Loss
and Letting Go

Working with people, I have found certain principles of letting go. The first is that the stages of mourning can take a minute, a year or a lifetime to complete. How long it takes is not dependent on outside circumstances. How long it takes, how fast or how slowly the process goes, depends on us. It is our right to decide how long the mourning process will be, as it is our experience and our loss. I have known people who decided to complete the mourning process in a minute. This was a beautiful and courageous minute and, at the end of it, they were ready to go on with their lives, having integrated the experience of the relationship. I have also seen people who refuse to let go, who rail against the present and hate the future, wanting only to go back to the way it was. Angry with life and with God, at the one who left them and ultimately at themselves, they are closed off to life and to what it offers them. If we refuse to let go, we will take on one of these self-defeating roles: dependence, independence or the untrue helper.

Letting go can take months or even years, and during this time, we can feel depressed, enervated, melancholic, sad and not our usual attractive selves. Until we let go, we are, in our minds, continuing in relationship with our ex-partner, and therefore have no openness to anyone else. Sometimes, out of anger or pain, we slam the door to relationships, and no one seems to appear until we realise what we have done, and decide to open it again.

The most powerful principle I have found about letting go is this: when we let go, something much better comes to take the place of what was lost. This principle extends to people and situations. When the attachment or fantasy has been released, there is an emptiness that can be filled. There is room for new life. Nature abhors a vacuum. When we let go, we allow ourselves to put things in proper perspective, so we can begin again by living in the present.

Exercise

I.   Today, spend about 10 minutes reflecting on the principle that when you let go something better comes to take its place. From time to time throughout the day, consider this in terms of your present situation.

II.   Today, go through memorabilia of the relationship . . . papers, clothes, gifts, pictures or whatever. Put these in order. Throw away what needs to be thrown away, and pack anything that needs to be put away, in order to allow you to put things in their present perspective. As you clean up and clean out, experience your emotions. This releases the past and helps you to come into the present.

WAY 6   The Stages of Letting Go

There are identifiable stages that we all go through in letting go. As you read, use the description of the stages to recognise where you are, and to prepare for the next step. You are being asked to let go. This shows that you are working through dependency and neediness. It is most important that you are honest with yourself or your denial will cause you pain. If you pass these tests in letting go, you can regain the relationship at a whole new level. The paradox is that if you let go to accomplish 'winning back' a partner, you aren't letting go. You must let go as if they will never come back. Only then will it work and all of your power and attractiveness be returned.

There are some principles that are particularly helpful when a relationship ends, such as: 'Do not call them.' This is a situation where your neediness will try to take, usually under the guise of giving. Phone vampirism will hurt your case and lower your attractiveness. You will know when you have succeeded in letting go in the first stage when they have called you. If you have abused the phone, they will not call until the second stage.

The first stage of letting go involves releasing all of the pain, needs, hopes, attachments, expectations, plans, desires, loneliness, etc. This is the toughest stage. When a partner calls, you have reached the first test at the end of the first stage. The reason they are calling is that they can feel your attractiveness growing through your letting-go. You are typically still at a vulnerable stage, but if you have awareness, determination and the balance of connection without need or attachment, you can save a whole level of letting go the long hard way. Stay as connected and detached as possible. Connection means being present and available to enjoy the call, but that is all. Being detached means you don't build up any hopes or fantasies. You enjoy the present moment completely, but don't make anything out of the call other than the pleasantness of the call itself. If you don't try to grab your partner through the phone, and you remain relaxed and unneedy, you will pass this test. If you past the first test, your partner will talk of going out or calling again; what's more, they will actually follow through on this if you are unattached to it happening. If you flunk it you will crash and burn and return to the place of pain where you began; you'll also have to start letting go all over again. You can't lie about how well you did in this first test. If you succeed you will feel fine and they will call back. If you are dramatically successful, you will be invited out to a public place for a date. It's a public place because your partner still won't be sure whether or not you will make a scene and a public place is the best way to ensure a normal evening.

By the time you reach the stage of accepting a date at a public place, you are at the test at the end of the second stage of letting go. By doing so well on the first test, which is enjoying the phone call but being unconcerned that anything comes of it, you can pass all the way up to the second test. If this doesn't happen, but you still passed the first test, you will need to let go of every bit of pain or loss that comes up in the second stage. It's just like the first stage but usually not as intense or painful. If they promise you a date or they promise to call, it will happen, but if and only if you have let go of the *need* for it to happen. If you get attached to them calling or to keeping their promises about the date, it won't happen. As soon as you become dependent or attached, you'll be back to stage one. They will cancel. If you become somewhat attached, they will postpone. Only when you are unattached will it come about. Always keep in mind that they can feel, no matter how great the distance, how much you are holding on and how much you are attached.

Letting go is better than a make-over. It is a powerful tool for bringing about the return of all of your attractiveness. If you let a person go completely, it is also a strong aphrodisiac. They will feel that they simply have to have you and be with you again.

Holding on is like taking 'ugly pills' – you will remain completely unattractive. I have seen this work hundreds of times over the 'air waves' . . . One friend, in a powerful letting-go exercise in a workshop, let go of two ex-wives and five ex-girlfriends. The next day he heard from all seven of them saying, 'Hey, big boy, come up and see me when you get home, wink, wink.' He had come from the US to take this workshop in Tokyo and they'd all taken the trouble to find him, feeling and knowing exactly when his attractiveness came back. He happily looked them all up when he returned from his visit to Japan.

When you go out, the key is to enjoy yourself, staying unattached but connected. Have fun and be carefree, letting go of any needs as they occur. Your stock rises as every time you do so. If you flunk the test you will 'crash' emotionally and have to begin letting go all over again from the very beginning. If you flunk it partially, they will promise to call. If you pass the test you are in stage three, they will make other dates. They will even keep those dates if you practice letting go more. If you pass this test with flying colours, they will invite you home with them that night. If you do not do so well, they will only promise to call. If you do poorly, they'll get away from you as quick as possible, you will crash and burn and have to start over, just as you did if you flunked the phone test. When you go home with them, enjoy yourself fully but don't get attached or imagine anything else happening other than what is happening then and there. Make nothing out of going home with them, even going to bed with them. Enjoy yourself, but be as unattached as you would on a one night stand. If you stay unattached, enjoying yourself like there's no tomorrow, going home with them could become a regular thing.

As you learn to let go of the last bits of the attachment to your relationship as it was, your relationship can have a new beginning. If you have only let go part way at this stage they will typically have another partner, but want to date you as well. At this point you have almost fully succeeded. Do not stop letting go now. If you agree to date while dating another you will be caught in a triangle relationship, one of the great traps to stop intimacy, love, and going forward. Do not get caught in a choice between two people. It is a trap. Choose the truth. Commit to the next step. Continue to let go of both. Remember that your true partner will join you at the next step, with the qualities of both people and you will know that what has happened was meant to be. If you keep letting go, they will either step up to become your true partner or someone new will come into that role because you have successfully let go.

Stages of Letting Go

Stage 1: Letting Go
Test: Your partner will phone

Stage 2: More Letting Go
Test: Date

Stage 3: More Letting Go
Test: Home to bed

Stage 4: Letting Go
Test: Your partner has another partner

Stage 5: The Final Letting Go
Which leads to renewal of relationship at a higher level

or

A new relationship at a higher level

If you let go very successfully during any test, you immediately go to the next step.

Exercise

Make a graph of all the stages and mark on it where you are. This will help you to become aware of the stages and the opportunity to jump from test to test, saving a lot of time. It will also help to know what to expect. Consider why and where you are in the stages. Commit to success at the stage you are in, and also for the following stages.

WAY 7 Happiness Is a Choice

Our minds process thousands of thoughts a day, all of which not only colour our perceptions, but actually make up or 'create' the world we see. Our minds contain thousands of beliefs, all of which have the power to choose how we view our world. Our beliefs are old decisions, assumptions and judgements about the world around us, and they dictate our present perceptions. Other factors that determine what happens to us or what we experience are the stories that we constantly tell about our lives. Some of them are dark, most of them are forgotten, but all of them become the scripts by which we live.

We have also set up conspiracies to remain in hiding, mainly because of our fear about who we really are and what our purpose is. Conspiracies are traps set up so well by the ego that it appears that we will never break free. Other complications that hold us back are our indulgences, addictions and idols, and deluding illusions that something outside us can bring us happiness. We have shadow figures and negative self-concepts, areas of self-attack and self-hatred, all of which are defences against our true goodness and wholeness. All of these are the mistaken choices that we thought would bring us happiness. Any negative event in our lives is a mistaken choice about what we thought would make us happy.

It is time to become aware of our choices, especially those that were made in a split second and then repressed. Without taking responsibility for our choices, we will never take responsibility for our lives or our happiness. We will think life is something that happens to us. If we are not happy, we believe that happiness has somehow evaded us. If we do not take responsibility for our happiness, enhancing what is working and healing that which is not working, then there is not much chance that we will be happy. If we are not always heading towards happiness, keeping it as our goal and our measuring stick, it is easy to wander off the path of happiness. We can look back through our life at our history of unhappiness. These are all the mistakes we made while looking for happiness in all the wrong places.

It is time to choose our happiness day and night. It is time to commit to happiness, knowing it is the most important thing. Happiness must include us in life. Happiness is not some mistaken notion of being in sacrifice now and being happy later. Happiness keeps things honest. If we are not happy now, or healing ourselves to become happy, we are making a mistake. This is not withstanding the grave challenges we sometimes go through, but the choice for happiness points to the successful outcome of these challenges. Evolution measures how much love and happiness we have in spite of it all. How could it be otherwise and still be evolution? How could it be otherwise and be love, light, spirituality and the legacy of Oneness?

Happiness is a choice on which we must concentrate. Nothing else will really work. When we make mistakes, it is crucial that we learn from them or our suffering will increase. If we are not responsible for our happiness, then we are at the mercy of a merciless world. We look out at the world, never knowing that what we see is derived from the choices we have made and are making now. We are, then, forever a victim, never climbing above this most powerless stance in life. If we do not think we have any power about how the world is, we may as well keep a low profile, attempting to keep ourselves and all those we love safe from the twists of fate. If we try to hide we live a shrink-wrapped life, we live defensively rather than expansively, and it is only by living expansively that we can be happy.

If we are not happy, something has become more important to us than happiness. We made a choice for something we thought would make us happy other than for happiness. What we chose did not make us happy, though we thought it would. So many of the things we thought would make us happy, that our ego assured us would make us happy, just did not work.

We can learn from and correct many of the choices that had unhappy outcomes, so we no longer make the same mistakes. We can learn that we have the power to become aware of our thoughts, so that we can make the choice to know, acknowledge and learn from our mistaken choices. We can learn that we have the power to choose for ourselves and improve our track record for happiness.

In the face of challenging circumstances, it is important to choose happiness and to ask for inner guidance to manoeuvre us into happiness through the challenges and temptations that are there to stop us. There is always a way if we are willing to change. If we are unhappy and do not choose to change and to heal fear, we begin to die. Happiness brings us life, which we naturally want to share with others.

Exercise

Make happiness the chief criterion for your life. Examine the incidents in your life as more than something that just 'happened' to you. Imagine you chose those things. What purpose would they have served for you? What were you trying to get out of having them occur? What did they allow you to do? What did you not have to do? Who were you trying to defeat and what were you trying to prove? What excuse did they give you? These are only some of the few mistaken wishes and choices we make when we think that something, other than happiness, will bring us happiness.

Desire happiness with all your heart. *Choose happiness for those you love, especially those that need you. The people around you who are unhappy reflect hidden pockets of your mind that are still caught in unhappiness. Choosing happiness for them helps you both.*

Every night before you go to sleep, choose happiness for your next day. Choose it again when you wake up. Choose it whenever you think of it. Choose it in the face of unhappiness. In spite of circumstances and for no good reason, choose happiness. It is the final truth, and it will make you feel at home, while showing you the way home.

WAY 8 'Burning' Emotion as a Form of Letting Go

There is a simple form of healing, a simple form of letting go. My wife Lency, who recognised, named and refined the method, calls it 'burning'. It is an apt name. Given any sort of willingness, this is both simple and effective. We simply feel what we are feeling. As we experience our feelings, which include pain, guilt, emptiness, blackness, deadness, numbness or blocked feelings, things begin to unfold to other typically deeper and worse feelings. But, when we have the courage, we experience these feelings and move through them to neutral and then to joyful feelings.

Suppressing emotions disassociates us and makes us independent instead of interdependent. Suppressed emotion automatically becomes stress. When we suppress emotion, the emotion itself becomes lost energy and it takes *additional* energy to keep the emotion suppressed. This loss of energy can cause us to become and remain tired and even depressed. Of the people I have worked with, the great majority who have suffered catastrophic illness had great caches of buried emotion inside. Releasing this energy does not kill us, but keeping it inside us might.

These emotions are layered inside us like tunnels going deeper and deeper until we are finally past the painful feelings and into the joy. But later we may stumble on another layer, or another tunnel of feeling. It is important to know that feeling or experiencing emotion does have an end and it will not go on forever. An added benefit of burning our emotions is that, as we burn them, we re-associate with our feelings. When we move into deeper layers, we not only re-associate with our feelings, but also with our body, sexuality and spirituality. As we open ourselves to feeling, we open ourselves to the same extent to receiving and relationship.

After a loss, we experience a glut of feeling. It is a very good time to reconnect with the painful feelings at hand. Simply experience, dig down to feel what is there to feel, exaggerating or leaning into the feeling, so as to move forward at an accelerated pace. Any feeling that is less than joyful can be grist for the mill. It just takes the courage to feel and we then begin to make progress.

Exercise

Today, spend as much time as you can experiencing your feelings. You can burn emotions and do almost anything else at the very same time. So, burning can be a background or undertone to anything else you are doing, such as eating or working. You can even tell yourself that you will continue burning in your sleep. Burning is a good basic healing method. Some people find this is their favourite method. Given some willingness and courage, it will move anything. As this method progresses, there seems to be a natural evolution towards grace and love.

WAY 9 Goal-Setting and Trust

One of the antidotes that relieves and releases holding on is goal-setting. Setting goals for ourselves takes away the pressure of expectations or demands we place on ourselves. It also sets up a flow, to move us from the place where holding on has kept us stuck. We set goals for where we want to be in a year, in six months, in three months, in a week and even by tomorrow. We move towards this goal as best as we can. If we find we have not reached our goal, or we have missed it, then we just reset the goal. Where is it you want to be by tomorrow? What is it you want to be feeling by then? How do you want the world to look to you? What do you want others to see when they look at you? Would you like to be able to bless your ex-partner when you think of them instead of feeling the knife in your heart? When you can bless your partner, you are equally blessed and your life is moved forward.

Trust, one of the core healing principles, helps both with setting goals and with letting go. Trust is acknowledging the power of our minds. Our mind is such that its power has to back something, and you get to decide what it backs. Trust is consciously putting our energy behind something, knowing it will work to our benefit, no matter how it looks now. The power of our mind can go towards fear or distrust if that is the direction we turn it in, or it can move towards trust and unfolding things directly to our benefit.

When we goal-set, the power of our mind works to help us reach our goals easily. It could take a few minutes of just concentrating, imagining and putting our energy behind the realisation of our goal. This means visualising, or experiencing it, as if it is already accomplished. Similarly, in letting go, trust helps us easily to bear the moment of empty-handedness experienced just after we let go. But, just as nature abhors a vacuum, our empty hands are soon filled in a happy way. Trust in letting go. Trust in what is coming next. When we trust, good things happen. Trust is not naiveté that overlooks denial; it actively supports positive unfolding through the power of our hearts and minds.

Exercise

Today, set goals for the next year. Every day examine your goals, especially the one for the day at hand. Recognise to what level you have succeeded. Then, reset your goal for the next day, paying particular attention to letting go. Bring your trust to your letting-go and to your goal-setting. Trust yourself. Trust your ex-partner, and trust any other significant players in your drama.

The Difference between Love
and Need – If It Hurts,
It Isn't Love!

When we feel heartbroken because we lose someone, most of us use our suffering as a measure of our love. But this simply is not true. Loving does not hurt, needing does.

We all have needs, at least this side of enlightenment. Our level of maturity is actually the level at which we handle our needs. Immature forms of handling needs include anger, hurt, emotional blackmail, revenge, indulgence, addiction, complaining, attack, withdrawal, dependence, independence, enabling, dissociation, pouting, 'vampiring', taking, manipulation, coercion, control, holding on, power struggles, competition, deadness, tantrums and glamour (that which calls for attention or seems to make us 'special' by trying to have more, either positively or negatively, than our fellow human beings). Every loss we release adds to our wisdom and maturity. Handling our needs wisely through communication, openness and responsiveness allows us to continue to evolve. Voraciousness, denial or embarrassment does not allow for growth.

It is important to know that the suffering aspect of what you are experiencing is not true love but merely an expression of needs. This can save you both the glamour of suffering, and the illusion of love. Many times, what we label as love is merely the 'specialness' in a relationship. If it hurts, it is your sense of 'specialness', being 'special', that has suffered. In truth, only your ego can suffer. You do not need to feel that way. If there is pain, it merely means that your ex-partner did not live up to the script you assigned to them. They broke rules that you had established for them in the relationship. Letting go of your needs allows you to receive and experience the love and connection that is there. When you are needy, you try to take but cannot receive. When you feel hurt because your partner seems to be pushing you away for no good reason, it is because you are giving to take. If you are not trying to take, you cannot be pushed away because love and wholeness do not make demands.

Exercise

Today, reflect on your present situation along with the suffering you experienced in your family and in your past relationships. Use the idea of 'love' instead of 'needs' to motivate you, to let go of as much of your past and present suffering as possible. If the past still seems bad or painful, the pain is not merely in the past but is still being carried on in the present. By letting go you can simply and easily free yourself, so that something much better can fill your mind and your life. Today, let go of the needs so love can fill your life.

WAY 11 Do You Love Someone Enough to Let Them Go?

A true test of our love is whether we love someone enough to let them go. Love is an ever-expanding blessing, a forever well-wishing, extending to another even when it does not seem to serve us. Do you love someone enough to wish the very best for them even if that does not include you? Or do you wish to possess them, hold them hostage against their will? It takes courage and trust to let someone go, and that courage and trust comes about through your love.

Would you hold against someone their desire to be somewhere else? To control someone is to watch them lose their spirit and attractiveness. Your only forward movement is to let them go. Paradoxically, only then is it possible for them to return to you. You cannot let someone go in order to bring them back, for letting go to bring someone back is a form of holding on. It just will not work. Letting go must be made with the purpose of living the truth, which is always living in the present, and not trying to foreordain what the truth is. Only through letting them go is there a possibility of bringing back a loved one, but for this to happen, you must wholeheartedly let them go, as if they will be gone forever from your life.

It may be that the best gift you have to give

your ex-partner is to let them go. Otherwise, your attachment would energetically hold them back, while, paradoxically, pushing them away from you. Simply said, you are using them to hold yourself back. Your ex-partner becomes your best excuse not to move forward and make something of your life. But, at the end of your life, what it has become is what you made of it, in spite of the challenges. By the end of your life, your excuses won't matter.

Whatever wonderful things this relationship has provided in your life, would you use it as a trap now? Would you use this time as a monument to your loss or would you use this time to celebrate the love and gifts you have received for however long the relationship lasted. Your relationship is over. There may or may not be another chapter with this particular partner; however, you need to accept that this part is over. The only way to tell if your ex-partner is in future chapters is to let go of this one. Reading a chapter over and over, no matter how good it was, keeps you from going on to the next chapter. And, if you dictate that this is the end of the book of your life, you make it a rather feeble ending, no matter how good it was before.

Exercise

Today, take a good look at how much you love your ex-partner. If you love them: set them free. Otherwise, look at how much your needs want you to enslave them and you in what would be a facsimile of a loving relationship. You have a chance today to choose love or neurosis. Love will let them go. What will you do?

Happiness is a state of mind invested in love, purpose, creativity, joy and heaven. Stubbornness is a suspicious state of mind, interested in fighting or resisting until it gets over its fear or gets its way. Stubbornness is a minor form of tantrum that digs in its heels to fight for what it wants. While happiness is open and seeks the truth, stubbornness just wants to be right, and it is impossible to have both stubbornness and happiness.

Our righteousness is usually a compensation, a defence against feeling guilty, so we get very stubborn about our position. Because the guilt threatens to come out with little provocation, we blame and judge others, or demand that our idea or ideal is the right way, the only way. Happiness just wants to find out the best way, and it is equally happy no matter who has the answer. In stubbornness, we identify ourselves with our position, and feel threatened or attacked if that position is questioned.

As we evolve from being adamant, our stubbornness takes the form of a role, or being stuck in an aspect of our character. While an aspect of character, such as working hard, may look quite successful, because it is a role we never receive or enjoy a reward. Our roles cover feelings of grievance for not being cared for better as a child, which in turn cover deeper feelings of failure and guilt about not saving our families. The purpose of a role is to demonstrate how care should have been given for us. Our roles are out to prove something. Both stubbornness and roles prevent us from receiving, despite all the hard work we do. We either block receiving any reward, or we spend what we receive to battle with stress. When we receive money or good things, they go out as fast as they come in, and provide little ease or refreshment. So our character, which we formed out of roles, seemed successful when we were children but becomes unresponsive, inauthentic, hard or heavy as armour, the older we get.

Roles create difficulty, and we feel caught in a rut and eventually burn out as a result of them. Happiness allows us to receive from our giving. It is the by-product of giving and of love. It refreshes us and allows us to savour the enjoyment. Stubbornness has an agenda. It wants to prove that we are right, so we do not have to deal with our feelings of being wrong, which in turn hide our fear of our need to change. Whenever we invest ourselves in an agenda or some job, then love, happiness and success are no longer the most important things. The job we have taken on takes priority, which does not always leave enough time for love, or overlooks happiness as secondary to getting the job done. Success becomes lost in our desire to cross something off our 'to-do' list. We somehow think that getting this job done will make us happy, while all the time we are proving what we believe to be right and hiding our stubbornness and fear. Of course, what we really believe we don't need to prove, and stubbornness hides our fear of moving forward.

Sometimes this stubbornness extends to becoming a victim. As part of proving that we are right, we become hurt in some way. 'See, this proves you are a bad person.' Or, 'Now I know for sure that you do not love me,' or 'See, I told you I was sick.' Somehow we think that once we have incontrovertible proof, at least in our own mind, of our righteousness, we will be happy. Our stubbornness is some kind of inflexibility, some attachment of which we refuse to let go, some over-burdening loyalty that ignores the truth.

Finally, stubbornness can be an attitude of resistance built out of fear and conflict with authority. As with any negative attitude, this turns us toward death. Because we reap what we sow, our lives become sour and bitter rather than generous and exultant. We have invested in the wrong things in life and this has led to scarcity (see page 195) and unhappiness. It is time to re-evaluate our lives and to give up our bad investments. If we can graciously admit where we are making mistakes, and take responsibility for them, we win back the attractiveness that comes with honesty and 'response'-ability to others. We allow for the flow of that which would truly make us happy. Our responsiveness to the truth, to others, and to life, generates a magnetic attractiveness for love, friendship, success and all the good things of life. On the other hand, stubbornness shuts down our minds, stops the flow of fun and opportunity, 'turns-off' partners or potential partners, and closes us off to success. Stubbornness has the answers, so it does not want to be confused by the facts. Most stubborn people consider themselves to be strong-willed, while others tend to think of them as the south ends of north-going mules. Stubbornness closes us off to grace or guidance from within, or input from outside, refusing to research, examine or explore; as such it is closed off from life.

Exercise

Where are you stubbornly clinging to a style or way of doing things that harms you? If you look closely at an area in which you are not successful, you will find it. You can choose to let this stubbornness go now.

I.   Locate any area where you are stuck, feeling dead or have difficulty. This is another area where you are stubbornly refusing to go forward, clinging to some outdated role or form of sacrifice. It is a mistake and you can give up your investment in it.

II.   Look at an area where people are fighting or resisting you. This helps you to pinpoint an area of stubbornness to which you are clinging. You can make another choice.

III.   Check out any area where you think people are wrong, bad, evil, going to hell, or should all be 'taken out and shot.' This shows areas of inflexibility and defensiveness, but mostly it reveals buried feelings of guilt or failure. These feelings are not the truth, but ego ploys to leave you stuck. You can ask the truth to lead you to the mistake and correct it, winning back your innocence. Then you will see others as calling for help rather than as deserving of hell. Happiness knows that anything you wish on another you wish on yourself.

WAY 13 Taking the First Step

Taking the first step in the letting-go process can sometimes be the hardest, and things typically get easier after this point. It is usual to find we have our own favourite style in letting go. Even though a general style might serve us well, we may also find other exercises and methods helpful. Pain comes up layer by layer and, after a state of peace, an even greater layer of pain may surface. Sometimes, after a breakthrough, the situation seems worse instead of better as we go into deeper layers of pain. This can come up on anniversaries of really big losses, so six months, one year, two years, five or ten years later, a new layer might emerge. When we are in a bad mood, but have no sense of what it is, we can trust our inner healing mechanism for timing. If we ask our intuition what the pain in our lives has to do with this bad feeling, we will find an answer. We may discover that, in every new stage of evolution we reach, one of the painful events of our life is coming up to be healed at different layers.

Often, layers and layers of pain come up, not so much because there is that much pain, but because the person involved is afraid to suffer anything new, being more willing to trust the devil they know than the one they do not. In this fear to trust and move forward in life, they use this 'manufactured' pain as a means to keep themselves back. It is important to recognise that when we have such a refusal going on, it is the result of a fear of going on with life. No amount of therapy or other methods will seem to work, because we are manufacturing pain as quickly as the therapy or letting-go process may be trying to clear it. This is the time to resolve and commit to taking the first step. If we find ourselves malingering, it is important to set goals for letting go. On a bad day, we can set very small goals. We will be energised and moved forward every time we complete a goal.

Exercise

I.   Every grievance stops you by anger, withdrawal and subconscious guilt. And every loss is connected with a grievance, for sadness and guilt go hand in hand. So say out loud: 'I forgive you (name of person) for my grievance. I will not use this to hold myself back.'

Do this over and over again with specific grievances. You may find that other people also come to mind in order to be forgiven; for example, past relationships, parents, friends, etc. Do this exercise with them as well.

II.   Clean out the paraphernalia of a relationship that now no longer fits your life. It may be important to take down any pictures of you with this person, at least until the letting-go process is finished. Clean out your handbag, briefcase, drawers, pantries, wardrobe, etc. You can do this with someone else's help, if that makes it easier.

III.   Make a list of incomplete projects. Let go of those that no longer fit your life. Reset goals for the ones which do fit.

WAY 14   Saying 'Yes' to Life

In the face of a great loss, the disappointment is often so strong that we withdraw from life, even to the point of killing the 'self' or 'personality' that was in charge of our mind. When this occurs, the mind is so prolific that a new self will come to take its place. However, when this occurs, we are also weakened, and become much more disassociated from ourselves. This means that our ability to succeed, receive and enjoy ourselves is greatly reduced.

When we have been battered by loss, we choose to withdraw. Our withdrawal leads to a loss of contact and joy. We feel unworthy, guilty and depressed. The extent of our withdrawal becomes the extent of our fear. On the other hand, the extent to which we are truly connected and bonded is the strength of our confidence. Each step forward builds confidence. If we do not let go, we limp through life as a shadow of our former selves.

Saying 'yes' to life marks our willingness for life to unfold, and is an invitation for the next step to begin. Taking the next step is not so much a literal striding forward as it is a willingness for life in its next phase to come to us. When there is this willingness, life seems to change significantly around us, typically within a two-week period. The next step in life is always better! Even though we do not know what it is, our willingness brings the next step to us.

Exercise

In this situation, the resolution to find a whole new level or chapter in your life simply awaits a sincere and heartfelt 'yes' to the next step, your willingness to step toward life and love rather than toward death.

List the three major heartbreaks you have had in your life. Ask yourself intuitively, on a scale of 1 to 100, how much of the problem you have left unresolved. The percentage you have not resolved reflects the loss or need that remains inside you; it is a place of withdrawal and continued pain. You can choose once again. You can say 'yes' to life in these situations, and by doing so have new aspects of life which have only been waiting for your invitation to come to you.

WAY 15 The Courage To Have the Feeling Change

A loss is a significant opportunity to step forward. In a mourning situation, many people do not want to change or to move because they are frightened to have the intense love they feel for the one they have lost change in any way. But it is important to recognise some principles that will help us to move forward. Again, most deep, intense, passionate love is more of a need/desire/urgency experience than a love experience. Love is, for the most part, a steadily radiating and ever-deepening experience. Secondly, if there is to be any hope for the relationship in the future, or at least the possibility of spending time with that partner again, these intense feelings have to change.

Even the sad feelings must change to those that radiate unattached brightness and expectancy towards life, not expectancy towards an ex-partner. We may even find we are not attached so much to the person of this ex-partner as we are to our feelings about the person, including the sadness.

I have had numerous clients who broke up with their partners and were deep in mourning. They seemed to have forgotten the fact that they created the separation themselves, or that it had been mutual. A few weeks after the break-up, they began to change the history of the break-up in their mind, and started to feel abandoned by their partner.

Once again, some courage is required to ensure that the feelings can run their cycle and finally come to one of peace. As peace and a feeling of detachment are reached (such as, 'It's OK if it works and OK if it does not, although I prefer it to work') then life will prepare itself to serve up our next lesson in relationships. As a new relationship or the next chapter in this relationship comes about, new feelings of romance and intensity naturally begin again.

Exercise

Use your present emotions as fuel for this exercise. It does not matter how positive, negative, tender or dead they seem to be. Make a work of art which symbolises the relationship. This could be in the form of a poem, collage, song, painting, story, drawing, dance or whatever form you choose. When you have finished it, if it is an object rather than a dance, then burn it, keeping only a photograph or copy if you want. If it is a real work of art, sell it or give it away rather than burn it. This exercise can be repeated as you feel inspired.

WAY 16   The Purpose and Length of the Relationship

Every relationship has a purpose. Part of that purpose will be the lessons that were learned in the relationship. The main purpose of every relationship is happiness. When we are not happy in a relationship, the purpose becomes healing. Every block between here and total enlightenment will come up between us and our partner. As we heal, more things come up to be healed. As we grow in confidence, we naturally become much more intimate, successful and happier, and able to deal with greater problems in ever-increasing creativity with each other.

Besides healing the blocks in our minds, there seems to be a special function that each relationship can fulfil – it's own contribution to the world. It also seems that within each relationship there is the power to *save* the world. Relationships are a continuum of healing and happiness. The evolution that takes place in a relationship helps and inspires more and more people. The healing that occurs between two people, and the love that grows, encourages new answers to come into being. Love is one of the best sparks of creativity. The further we progress in our own healing, the more we are shown the way for our own natural leadership.

Every relationship on this earthly plane has an ending. The relationship may last for only a short time or for a lifetime. Lifetime relationships normally take place when we find a suitable partner with whom we can learn lesson after lesson together. Then, there are those relationships that last for a shorter duration, perhaps to learn a certain lesson, or to enjoy a certain time together. In addition to these, there are the seemingly chance and brief encounters, which are also purposeful, if short-lived.

Sometimes the purpose of a relationship is only to get us in touch with a hidden block or conflict. At other times, one relationship may be there just to get us ready for another lifetime relationship ahead.

Exercise

Ask your intuition what the purpose of your relationship was and trust whatever seems to pop into your head.

If nothing seems to pop in, reflect further on the possibilities throughout the day.

Ask your higher mind (see page 194) today to show you what the purpose of your relationship was, and to help in the easy completion of any unfinished purpose that stems from it.

WAY 17 Saying Goodbye

It is very helpful to be able to share with an ex-partner and to say good-bye. It's also useful to have a summary of that relationship put into perspective in the context of our lives. It helps to tell a person what a relationship has meant to us, although, sometimes, because of death, or another abrupt departure, we are not able to have this communication. Again, it is not recommended that you call someone who has broken up with you; you may try to 'vampire' them under the guise of letting go, but because of your denial you will have no realisation as to why the call did not work. If your ex-partner has not contacted you, it is best to do this part of the letting-go on your own. Over 25 years ago, in response to a friend who had lost her beloved through cancer, I had an inspiration that has helped many people in the termination process. If you are not in direct communication with your ex-partner, you may wish to write a letter or to get into a candlelit bath and speak to him or her either out loud or in your mind. You may find this easiest to do in a meditative setting with soft music playing in the background.

Exercise

In whatever setting or medium you have chosen to do

his exercise, write to your ex-partner, or tell them out loud or in your mind, what you loved and appreciated about them. Often it helps to imagine or feel them present as you say these things.

Now share with them what did not work for you, where you are angry or feel incomplete.

Now share with them the best thing about the relationship, or the best thing that happened in it.

Share with them the most painful part of the relationship, and . . .

. . . the funniest thing in it

. . the saddest thing, or biggest loss, you experienced

. . . the happiest time in the relationship

. . . the thing that they gave you, which no one had ever given you before

. . . the most beautiful, tender part of the relationship to you

. . . the worst part of the relationship to you

. . . what gift they inspired or called out of you that you did not know was in you

. . . what lesson you learned with them

. . . what old pain or fear you got to heal through the relationship

Now imagine that you were writer, director and star in the relationship. What scene in the relationship would you rewrite to be better and how would you rewrite it? Are there other scenes you would like to rewrite like this, if only at a feeling level?

What was the part you regretted or felt guiltiest about?

What was the hardest thing through which you helped them and they helped you?

What is it you would like to thank them for, and thank God for them about?

WAY 18 Life Is What You Make It

Just as we are born with certain physical character-istics, we are also born with certain behaviour pat-terns that are either passed down to us ancestrally, or brought in by our soul to learn certain lessons. We are also born with certain gifts, talents and levels of consciousness that our souls have brought in their backpacks to help us to deal with the chal-lenges, lessons and traps that we have come to face and transform. As we heal our patterns, we can accomplish our purpose by giving our specific gifts, which were hidden by these patterns, to help our family and the world.

Yet our ego has other hidden agendas to make itself strong, to make us special, to win at all costs, and to have more than anyone else – even if this causes us to suffer and fail. Sometimes we fail miser-ably or suffer untold horrors, just to get attention and make a name for ourselves in some way. We must choose between our healing agenda or the ego's agenda of either aggrandising or shrinking itself.

For our life to be great we must overcome these early patterns and realise that the ego's plans just won't work. If we do not have what we want, if our life does not seem to be what we wish for, then it is time to become aware of the ego's hidden strategies that keep us from succeeding and to make new choices. The ego is made up of the principles of 'specialness', separation, competition, fear, guilt and the authority conflict. Only when we can melt the ego, can we find love, and create joy and happiness. The ego raises our fear, and tells us that its loss will mean our death, but in truth it is only the death of the ego. Success and abundance can only come about through peace and confidence, which is the opposite of how the ego builds itself – on right-eousness, domination, defensiveness, divisiveness, aggression, acquisitiveness and conflict. The ego tells us to identify with our body as ourselves. As a result we get frightened of death and shrink from truly living our lives.

To be happy, we must be responsible. Our life is what we make it, and our happiness is what we make it. If we are not happy, it is up to us to do something about it. We can continue to complain, but it won't change anything. Life presents every-one with challenges, issues and pain. We all have unlearned lessons and all manner of limitations. Yet we have all come to be happy. It is the experience of our spirit, which is the light, love and exquisite happiness that we all in truth seek. The happiness in our relationships is but an echo of what is available to us as we experience the spirit within all of us.

There are certain principles that bring about happiness, that melt the ego, open us to love, and even get us drunk on joy and bliss. On the other hand, there are dark stories that we make up, that we think will make us happy, which include stories and scripts of being unloved, or contain tragedy, revenge, heartbreak, guilt, martyrdom, tantrum, indulgence, malice and much more. When we examine these stories consciously we see that they are obvious mistakes. Besides dark stories, there are deluding passions and conspiracies that we use to hide ourselves and our purpose. There are shadow figures (see page 195) we use to hide our true goodness, our power and our innocence, thus abandoning our destiny and failing in our quest for happiness.

Yet happiness is simple. It is the means and the goal. It is how much we give, and how much we share ourselves. It is our choice whether we will meet the challenges, learn the lessons, and accept nothing less than the truth of happiness in our lives. Happiness comes from our openness, our willingness to join and partner, our receiving grace, our connection with our mind, heart, body and spirit, our reaching out to give our gifts, our surrendering to others, truth, life and God. Happiness comes about through our openness to receive the force of creativity as it pours through us, our willingness to let go, trust and move forward. Happiness also comes from the joy of learning, the freedom of unlearning what keeps us in pain, the bonding that gives us friends, and the truth that gives us meaning in a world of lies.

Happiness states that we reap what we sow, not just by actions, but by thoughts as well. If we invest positively and wisely, we cannot help but be happy. Anything less than this shows an unwise investment in what we think, believe, value, feel and do. While our world reflects our mistaken choices, all this can be changed. We can change our minds, learn where we are mistaken, and make new choices. We can use all negative emotions as an indicator that we are making a mistake, rather than displacing or taking them out on others. Let us use every painful situation to ascertain the mistaken choices and the bad investments that we have made so that we can correct them.

Blame and grievances towards others show our hidden guilt and unwillingness to take responsibility and to change. We want others to change to make us feel better, and it will not work. 'Response'-ability and responsibility are two of the principles needed for happiness. The fullness with which we embrace and love ourselves, embrace our destiny and life, is the extent to which we will be happy. Let us take ourselves lightly and see the humour in life. The ego hates laughter, unless it is derisive, but true laughter heals, balances and gives true perspective. To increase our happiness, we must share it with others.

Exercise

I   *Truthfully score yourself on the following:*
• *How happy are you?*
• *What choices would help you now to make yourself happier?*

II   *Today, examine a painful situation:*
• *What are the mistaken choices?*
• *What are the negative beliefs in which you have invested?*

- *What are the values that don't serve you?*
- *What are the self-concepts that have brought about the situation?*
- *What negative stories are you telling by this situation?*
- *Do you have conspiracies (see page 193) involved, traps so effective that you are never meant to get out of them? How do you think they serve you?*
- *What are you trying to get from the person or situation that is causing you pain?*
- *What are you afraid to receive that would clear all of this up?*
- *What mistaken guilt did you think you could pay off by having this happen?*
- *Besides your ex-partner, who are you trying to get revenge on by having this happen?*
- *Who are you trying to defeat by having this happen? How?*
- *What are you trying to prove or be right about in this situation?*
- *Let go of all these mistaken choices and investments.*
- *What would you choose now for your happiness?*
- *What would you choose now for your life?*

This Loss Hides a
Greater Loss

The greater the loss, the more it hides an older, deeper loss. This old loss was the root that blossomed into the fruit of this present loss. Many times a loss is hard to let go of because it is not just a single incident but a whole pattern. However, because of this, there is also an ability to heal the whole pattern by dealing effectively with the present loss.

What has consistently shown itself, while working with the subconscious in therapy, is that traumas in our lives do not just happen but have a precedent. And, the greater the present problem, the greater the original loss.

It takes great awareness and maturity to realise that everything happens for the best, particularly in our own lives where our first tendency after loss involves feelings of depression, valuelessness, fear, self-attack, failure, guilt and sadness. These are the very feelings that have, for the most part, already been buried within us, waiting for an opportunity to be finally transcended. One of the most surprising things I learned in therapy was that present feelings of pain were normally already in the subconscious, and the present situation was just the trigger for their emergence. There is actually very little of the emotion stemming from the present situation.

If we are totally unaware of the subconscious, we will mourn all of the past and present feelings under the aegis of the present loss. But it takes great awareness and maturity to realise this. One way to realise it is to complete the letting-go process. In this, you naturally understand what is past and what is present. And, as you do, the next level of your life begins.

Exercise

Consider your present loss: if a previous loss has not already occurred to you, ask yourself intuitively at what age the previous loss may have occurred. Then ask yourself who was present when the loss occurred. Ask yourself what it was that must have occurred in order for you to have created such a pattern of loss. In the original scene, ask yourself what everyone must have been feeling to act the way they did. Typically, there is a core painful feeling that everyone shared. It is the same feeling that is now part of your pattern. Now look at everyone in the scene, asking yourself how long they have had this pattern, where it began for them and how it showed up in their lives, as pain, or defence against pain, or both.

WAY 20 The Refusal to Let Go

A refusal to let go is often an indication that we are holding on to more than one person. This could mean that a dream or self-concept was shattered, or that a fusion or heartbreak reflecting the same experiences from childhood was involved.

The refusal to let go is malingering, and involves using the present loss as an excuse not to move forward. This pattern is at the heart of our conspiracy against our true self, our purpose and our greatness. It is using victimisation as an excuse not to move forward in a specific area that frightens us. We are concerned that we cannot possibly figure out what the next step is, or how we could accomplish it. But that is not our responsibility. Our responsibility is to be willing. With willingness we are moved forward, our fear is transcended, and the next step comes to us. We do not have to work it all out for ourselves. This serves only to delay us, being just another form of resistance and control.

When we are willing, anything accomplished is done through us, but not by us. Whatever we try to do ourselves, we do with graceless difficulty. With the attitude of 'not by us, but through us', we just need to show up; what we need to say or do will be given to us. This allows for grace, and bypasses control, which is generated by fear, old heartbreak and authority conflict. Our performance anxiety, our perfectionism, our feelings of inadequacy, our lack of trust that leads to control and fear, any competitiveness or sense of failure – which the deadness in our life hides – are all answered and transcended by letting things be done through rather than by us. The more we try to do everything, the more stress, difficulty and unnecessary hard work is created. And the more we try to do things, the more fear we feel about the future and the more guilt or failure we feel about the past.

Exercise

Every time you feel unhappy, it is a signal you were trying to do something. You can use the times you feel some kind of emotional pain as an opportunity to let go of a whole pattern of 'doing'. This allows for events to occur in an inspired way. Today, be willing to change or have changed for you any area on to which you have been holding in your last relationship.

Make a list of what you are trying to 'do' in your life. Items on this list will reflect areas of guilt, pain, failure, fear, insecurity, scarcity, difficulty and lack of success. 'Doing' blocks inspiration, creativity, ease, freedom and vision. Be willing to study the effects of letting this 'doing' go. Everything can be accomplished gracefully through, not by, you.

WAY 21 Holding On as a Cover for Fear

Holding on to heartbreak can be a cover for fear. When we are afraid of moving forward, when we do not have confidence for the next step, when we are afraid of success, sex, intimacy or marriage, we can disguise all of this by holding on to the partner we just lost. Sometimes this person will be the best thing that ever happened to us, or it may have been someone with whom we were only close for a short while; whatever the case, we have often idealised our emotion about the relationship. The amount of pain, sorrow and attachment we are experiencing may, in fact, be an overreaction, while the fear that may be hidden under all the other feelings is actually the strongest element in the holding on. If we recognise that the fear of change and the fear of losing the powerful feelings toward someone are key elements in our holding on, we will be much more aware of what needs to be dealt with as we move on. If we don't deal with the fear that is the underlying issue, causing us to hold on, we won't be successful in letting go.

The fear of change and moving forward is not just some idle fear, but one that is at the root of every problem that we have. When we are particularly frightened of moving forward for fear that we would lose something, or that the next step would be worse, or that something would be asked of us that we could not handle, then we disguise our fear of moving forward with some form of holding on. This can become chronic when we have disguised the real issue so well we do not really deal with it. Similarly, we're afraid that the vibrant, intense feelings we have toward our ex-partners may change. We want to keep them and this feeling as the central part of our lives. If we move forward the feeling will change, becoming far less a part of the urgent foreground and simply a natural backdrop. If we were willing to let go fully, someone even better suited to us will take the place of whomever it is we have released. Although there is no doubt that we will be happier in the long run, it is still difficult to trust in the future when we are experiencing deep (even if they are inauthentic) feelings now. If we do not let go we may keep urgent feelings about our dreams and memories but we will never have our perfect mate, as these very dependent feelings will chase them away.

Once we recognise what it is that frightens us, we can begin to let it go. Fear always has an object. If we are afraid of change and of the future we'll stay stuck in the past and our lives will never work. Only our willingness to go forward will succeed. Other ways to move through fear are by love, trust, choice, putting it in God's hands, forgiveness, letting go of the need, and giving up the judgement, attack and self-attack. Fear can also be healed when we recognise that we are not alone, and that God walks with us wherever we go.

Exercise

Today, appraise a problem situation as one of holding on. Is the attachment hidden or visible? If hidden, intuit or dwell on what it could possibly be. When you become aware of it, recognise that it has not been successful, and it has not made you happy. If you are willing, choose to let this go now. Paradoxically, as you let go, you move into the flow of life and you can receive once again.

Recognise that the fear of the next step is actually caused by a grievance you have with someone who you have not forgiven. Even as you read this, they will begin to come to your mind. Forgive them to be free. As you think of them, ask for their blessing. This can free you both.

Fear of the next step is the result of something you have with which you have not successfully come to terms in the past; therefore trying to rush into the future will not succeed until you weigh the anchor of the past. Rushing into the future – which is a compensation and takes an opposite form to holding on, while actually acting to cover it – is a way of hiding your fear of the future. It has the same dynamic as someone chasing a love partner who is actually chasing them away out of fear. Recognise your style of holding on. Do you tend to get depressed, rush into the future, or compensate for your loss by avoiding your feelings and helping others, acting needy or acting dissociated, as if you have no needs? Whatever your style, imagine yourself putting all of this in the hands of your higher mind. By doing this, you can let go of 'now' in order to move forward.

Fear can be released easily if we realise that we are

not alone, and that God walks with us. We can face anything, and any situation will become more inviting and less troublesome.

Another way to move forward once you have discovered your fear is to feel the fear until it melts away. Recognise that the feeling sometimes gets stronger when you give it attention. But, if you burn through the feelings until you become peaceful, you will free yourself to the extent that you are now able to move forward. Other layers may come up, but you can deal with them in the same way.

Willingness to move forward will also move us forward. The smallest willingness will allow our higher minds to empower us to begin moving forward once again.

WAY 22 Forgiveness as a Form of Letting Go

Forgiveness concludes unfinished business. It ties up loose ends and allows for a new beginning. Forgiveness releases the one we forgive as it releases us. It frees us from the paralysis that a grievance generates. It also frees us from the subconscious guilt that every grievance hides and that holds back our lives. There is virtually no one with whom we do not harbour some grievance or judgement. The amount of grievances we have, either apparent or subconscious, is the amount of pain, lack of success and scarcity (see page 195) in our lives.

As we forgive we find a new day dawning for ourselves, the beginning of a new chapter in our lives. Forgiving grievances releases the past and allows miracles to transform our lives. Every grievance we release, frees others and ourselves from the prisons and pain we are in.

Forgiveness seems to be the hardest lesson for human beings to learn. To accept forgiveness, it is necessary for us to let go of our righteousness. Our righteousness allows and justifies our being angry, ostensibly to defend ourselves, but actually to hide our guilt and pain and give us the excuse to do whatever we want. But our righteous, angry reactions do not allow the hidden guilt present under every grievance to be released. Only forgiveness can do this.

At the deepest level of the subconscious, we are in collusion with the person with whom we have the grievance. At some level their behaviour gives us the excuse we wanted. On the other hand, it also allows us to attack ourselves as a form of rebellion and revenge against partners, parents and God. Being aware of this collusion can help us heal by becoming aware of our hidden agendas. That allows us to face the buried reasons why we would seemingly act against our own best interests. We can end the self-deception, and empower ourselves by making new choices. For instance, sometimes we choose to be victimised to justify doing something we wanted to do all along, but otherwise would not have allowed ourselves to do. For example, if a partner has an affair, we use it to justify having an affair or getting a divorce, which was probably what we wanted to do all along. Once we know why we created certain events together and what the hidden agenda was on our part, it becomes much easier to forgive ourselves. As we bring each past pain to light and release it, we begin to see how important it is to use all of our conflicts for self-awareness and healing.

Forgiveness sets things straight and opens the door to living fully. It opens us once again to receiving the good things that life has to offer. Forgiveness gives us back our real selves, freed and successful, no longer buried in conscious grievances and subconscious guilt.

Our grievances lock us in a world of pain and revenge. Grievances are actually subconscious projections. We accuse others of doing what we are doing, though we deny this to ourselves and sometimes appear to act the opposite to the behaviour we are judging. Forgiveness frees us of this pattern and brings us back to the present. It helps us to get on with our lives instead of fighting a past that never really was, but simply remembered now to serve a certain purpose. This memory is our excuse to hide and to avoid facing our fears, especially the fear of our purpose.

Exercise

I.   Imagine the person with whom you have the grievance standing in front of you. Now, look beyond their mistakes, beyond their personality and beyond their body – just see, feel, sense or imagine the light that is their spirit inside them. Imagine your light joining with their light.

II.   Go back to a certain painful incident in your life. Do this same exercise with the people present, starting with the ones closest to you. Join your combined light with each succeeding person until you get to the one with whom you are most separated.

III.   Ask your higher mind to accomplish any forgiveness which may seem beyond you, bringing you the peace and understanding necessary for moving forward.

WAY 23 Happiness Is Letting Go of Grievances

We may think a grievance is about someone doing something wrong, but actually we are judging another because they are not acting in a way that satisfies one of our own needs. That need has a history. We have brought into the present a need that was not met in the past, and a conflict that occurred when the need began. If we went deeper still, we would find that the grievance and judgement we have against this person is really an old judgement on ourselves for something similar we felt we did and about which we feel some guilt. Every grievance we have comes from the past. We want someone to make up to us for this past grievance, before we are willing to let it go. Of course, we may wait till cobwebs grow over us trying to get someone, anyone, to make up for this old grievance.

A big part of the problem with a grievance is that we actually hold this grievance against everyone. The separation, withdrawal and attack will be paid for even by the people we love the most. Grievances make someone – and ultimately everyone – pay for our past.

Sometimes others have no idea that we hold a grievance against them because they are plugging away as best they can. A grievance makes us think it is someone else's job to make us happy. This is one of the biggest traps in relationships. The strategy of trying to get someone to satisfy our past needs simply will not succeed, except in the rare case that someone comes towards us with a whole new level of love and understanding. When we are attacking someone with our needs, yes, attacking them, it is only a matter of time before we are attacking them for either not meeting our needs ('They have plenty, I don't, and they are withholding from me, it is so unfair!') or for meeting our needs ('Just who does he think he is, and why is he acting like he's so much better than me?!'). We are cheating ourselves out of happiness now because of past grievances. If we went deeper into the past or subconscious, we would find that our grievances come from what we believe we did, in spite of the great story we have about it being other people's fault. Instead of all that we could have happiness now.

When the past is a problem because of grievances, the future becomes a problem because of fear. To be happy, to feel loved, we must let go of the grievances that keep us living in a past that never occurred, except in our minds. These grievances are actually a way of disguising profound feelings of failure and guilt, which are also mistakes on our part. Failure and guilt are grievances against ourselves, which are just as mistaken as grievances against others. This level of grievances against ourselves is meant to hide our true goodness and power.

Our guilt also keeps us living in the past and afraid of the future because we see the future as just being more of the same. That is why letting go of our grievances benefits us. When we let go of grievances with others, we let go of the self-attack and grievances against ourselves. We come back to the here and now, and the happiness that waits for us at the centre of life. We now have a rosier picture of our future and we feel peace about the past. This opens up the present to the eternal.

Our grievances keep us righteous and hide our guilt. All of this keep us shut down, obsessed, and living in a past that never quite took place as we registered it. When true understanding in the past takes place, we regain the lost bonding and the pain dissolves. Our ego uses our grievances for control and it does not mind twisting a few facts or triggering some buried emotion to make us angry and righteous. It wants us to avoid our present because the present melts the ego as a place of love and happiness. When we live in the past or the future, our egos keep themselves strong. Unless you are happy, you are only living in the past. When we live in the here and now there is less separation, more intimacy and success with people around us. We have all developed to the place where the ego is strong. Now it is time to learn to melt it away, and to let it be replaced by our higher mind. Only in this way can we be totally happy. Our ego is not interested in our happiness, but it is definitely invested in us being right, which keeps us stuck.

Letting go of the grievances moves us forward, past the righteousness and into receiving. When we recognise the ego's agenda in fighting peace and maintaining conflict, we will also recognise that we have an ability to reject this plan and to make a new choice. When we recognise the hidden, or not-so-hidden, elements of what we are blaming ourselves for in our grievance toward another, it allows us to forgive others and ourselves.

Our grievances are part of the ego's agenda to keep itself strong. It tries to convince us that grievances make us happy, but if we have spent any more than five seconds dwelling on a grievance, we know how bad it feels. The longer we stay in a grievance the worse we feel.

Exercise

It is crucial for us to make the choice:

Do we want grievances or happiness?

Do we want to miss the present, our only chance to be happy?

Or, do we want to try to keep remaking the past or running into the future trying to make it better, in an attempt to escape an unhappy past?

Today, make a choice to recognise the grievances that are keeping you from happiness and peace. Always look for grievances under any problem. You cannot have a problem without a grievance generating it, locking you in the past instead of finding the solution that waits for you in the here and now.

If you are now willing to have the answer and be happy, let go of the grievance.

If you are willing to win an ally instead of keeping an enemy, let go of the grievance and forgive.

If you are willing to leave the past and the future, and have the present, you can have your happiness and your effectiveness back.

A Refusal to Let Go Hides
the Fear of Fear

When we refuse to let go, our attachment is nothing more than a disguise and a defence to hide our fear. This is also true when we hold on to trauma and old relationships from the past. With the many issues we carry from the past, we can mask not only our fear but also our fear of fear itself. Fear shrinks and paralyses us, while the fear of fear shrinks us from dealing with what has paralysed us, as we start to deal with the issue at hand. Fear of fear makes our fear almost impossible to deal with because we run from it. This leaves us with a few unhappy choices: to quit, give up hope, or cover the fear with so much denial and whitewash that it's as if the fear doesn't exist for us. So, while the fear of fear is still affecting us, it remains so 'compensated for' (see page 193) and hidden that it is revealed only by the evidence that we're not moving forward. The alternative is to find the truth, the way through, the healing or miracle that exists for every problem situation.

Some people cannot tell the difference between the healing principle of letting go and throwing something away. If we get frightened of fear we either cower and become totally dependent, such as when we have an illness, or we abruptly throw our relationship away. Throwing away is an act of dissociation, or sabotage, as we undo all that we have put together. The fear of fear keeps generating more fear, which we then use to keep us more independent, or it incapacitates us so totally that we need outside support. When we are independent, we normally believe that we are not afraid of anything. Actually, the reverse is true, because often we are afraid of feelings, emotions, needs, relationships, intimacy, ourselves and our purpose. The way we deny what we are afraid of is a sure sign we have become afraid of fear. All of our unyielding attachment comes as a result of our fear of change or moving forward. However, the longer we stay attached, the more we become stuck and finally we become afraid of the fear itself. This may show itself as strong independence, paralysis, stubbornness or intransigence – all are fairly good indications of the fear of fear.

As we become bullied by fear, we resent people who seem to be bullying us to let go and move forward, for our own good. Actually, we are projecting our self-bullying on to them. When we are afraid, we take the fear as if it were real and live accordingly. Yet fear is an illusion that comes from lost bonding and the well of sadness inside us. As a result, we think that we are going to lose again, which causes us to shrink back from the future, from relationships and from ourselves, and dig in our heels. Yet the attachment, chronic as it may be, is just a cover for our fear of moving forward. If we keep going in the direction of attacking ourselves it can easily turn into a tortuous fear of fear. When we become frightened of our fear, we become frightened of exploring our minds, dealing with our fears, and seeing them as the illusion they are.

Fear is an illusion that comes from misunderstanding, reinforced by the separation and the misperception it generates. As we join and re-establish bonding through understanding, letting go, giving, receiving or forgiving, we realise that there has been a misunderstanding that can quickly be remedied. Because the fear is hidden under the attachment, if we become frightened of our fear, we will be emphasising the wrong issue because our fear limits our awareness. The more we try to force ourselves to let go, the more unsuccessful and frightened we will become. Fear at one level comes from self-attack. So our fear of fear is a level of anguish and self-torture. We become so afraid of suffering from our fear that we fail to notice that we are already suffering and still terrified.

We must get over our fear of fear before we can understand that the fear is the root issue and, as such, we will become successful only if we deal with it as the primary cause. Courage wouldn't be courage if we weren't frightened and still faced our fear. If we are willing to stop attacking ourselves with our fearful thoughts, we can more easily and successfully let go of the holding-on because it was just the 'cover' issue. We no longer deny our fear, but deal with it as an everyday, if illusionary, part of life. The courage and awareness to face fear heals the unwillingness and stubbornness that the fear of fear produces.

Exercise

Examine your life. Has there been an area in your life that you have blocked off and are not dealing with in part or as a whole? This could involve emotions, relationships, sex, success, money, career, family or numerous other specific issues. What or whom have you been holding onto? Are you afraid of dealing with the fear of moving forward? Examine the major setbacks from the past onto which you are still holding, and which sustain your fear of moving on. Include in this any problems, failures, losses or deaths, or any significant relationships. Reflect on those people or situations onto which you are holding as an excuse not to face your fear and go forward. If you are willing to face the fear, there is an easy way to do it now.

First, if you are too frightened to be willing, at least be willing to be willing. Your 'higher mind' (see page 194) needs only the smallest modicum of willingness on your part to help you move forward. It supplies the rest. It is why it is the higher mind. It is meant to handle our problems for us.

Choose a suitable room that is big enough for the exercise. Now find a symbol, something to represent each painful loss or person to whom you are attached. Put these in a line about 60cm (2ft) from each other across the room. Put these in the order of your choosing, such as chronologically, or the importance of that person to you, or degree to which you are holding on to them. Include any traumatic situation that could still be holding you back. Remember, fighting or grievances against anyone are just a way of holding on to someone in a negative fashion. They still hide your fear and they have become an excuse to not move forward.

Some people find that just hunting for the perfect object to symbolise each person or event is helpful. Others can't be bothered with things and do the whole exercise in their imagination. Whether you are doing it with symbols or in your mind, or simply visualising the actual people or events that you intend to let go, put something at the other end of the line in the room that symbolises trust for you. Imagine all of these attachments are between you and the trust and the letting go of these attachments will heal your fear of fear.

Step forward and take the object in hand or merely visualise the first person or situation to which you are attached. When you are willing no longer to use this person or event to hold yourself back, imagine yourself letting it go or putting it in the hands of God. Then step forward to the next symbol, person or situation. See the attachment in your mind's eye once again. When you are no longer ready to use this to hold yourself back, let it go. It will fall into perspective in your life. Let go of each attachment until you have let go of everything between you and trust. Each of those attachments represented a place where you were frightened to move forward. Each letting go heals a level of fear.

As you embrace trust and its symbol feel the power of it filling you giving you the courage to move forward.

WAY 25 This Loss Hides a Place of Sacred Fire

Sacred Fire is a place in the unconscious mind where two great fractures of the mind are held apart by some major pain. Sacred Fire refers to heart-wrenching pain that hurts so bad we feel tempted to die. In actuality, this place of great pain can easily be transformed to high levels of love, creativity and power. We have already said that any major loss is partly the result of previous loss or heartbreak so severe and painful that, were we to live it again, it would take us to our knees. This is an area of the mind I call Sacred Fire-Pain or Sacred Fire-Purification.

People will go into rage rather than allow themselves to experience that much pain. Or, there is the usual ploy of trying to run away from it, or attacking the person closest to us. 'If I am hurting this bad, it must be their fault!' Ultimately, these defences do not work and this pain, rightly seen or dealt with, signals birth, not death.

What happens is that two major fragments of the mind that were fractured in some past trauma are now coming back together. All the pain that kept them apart is coming up. The dire emotions of Sacred Fire-Pain are heartbreak, jealousy, terror, futility, uselessness, hopelessness, anger/rage/violence, desperation, despair, nothingness, emptiness, loneliness or the feelings of being completely lost and cursed. Again, Sacred Fire-Pain is identifiable because of the high degree of pain. We feel knocked to our knees. Awareness is one of the key ways to escape from such dire pain. As soon as we implement the simple yet profound solution, the pain is transformed. It is a degree of pain so profound, distracting and consuming that, at times, we can even forget that we know the solution. The pain is actually a form of purification that, as it is experienced, brings about the integration of those parts of the mind fractured in the trauma. Only those most advanced emotionally can feel through this level of emotion until it becomes a new birth. Most of us find a way to turn away from the pain, leaving ourselves unbirthed, still fragmented and once again dissociated.

Through giving, the pain is transformed into Sacred Fire-Birth, or one of its other forms, such as high level gifts of vision, purpose, creativity, art, healing, sexuality, beauty, true love or psychic ability in some form. It can even open shamanic powers of healing or ability to transcend some of the laws of time and space. So, from a place of withdrawal and constriction, we can reach a new level of greatness, confidence and power.

Exercise

As soon as you realise you are in Sacred Fire-Pain, you need only give or step through the pain to help someone. It may help to imagine a ring of fire you are stepping through to help someone. You might ask who needs your help, seeing them on the other side of the ring of fire.

Would you be willing to step through your pain for them? Because if that person is the one who appears to you, he or she is probably in even more dire circumstances or pain than you are, although at an obvious level this may be disguised. If helping them is more important than your pain, step through that ring of fire to help them. As you step through the fire just embrace them, feeling your love and support pass into them. This is usually enough to end all of the pain. If any is left, ask once again and repeat the exercise.

Today, with any pain you feel, ask yourself to whom you are called to give and how. It may be as simple as sending loving thoughts or blessings to someone. It may be calling or contacting them in some way. Or it may even be a creative project that would be a gift to many people.

Today, your giving transforms your pain to a new birth of creativity and love.

Letting Go of the Good,
Letting Go of the Bad

In a letting-go situation, we first let go of what was bad and then let go of what was good in the relationship. Primarily, we recognise we are holding on and caught up in what was painful about the relationship. We work on the problems, bad feeling and grievances. But, after a while, these seem to fall into perspective and they are no longer as pressing or painful. We have moved through the pain and somehow have resolved that which held us back. Now what comes up is something entirely different, unless the relationship was entirely negative. We find ourselves thinking about all of the good things. And it usually is harder and takes longer to let go of what we loved. Maybe it is because we are so used to the bad things in a relationship, that the good things seem harder to come by. In most relationships, it is the good that is held on to most tightly, long after the other partner has gone. Often, after a death, a partner idealises the late partner, almost raising them to sainthood. Sometimes, we can tell what stage of the letting-go process we are in just by knowing whether we are working on letting go of the bad things of the relationship or on the good things.

While it is important to resolve and let go of

the negative, so that a pattern is not created, it is also important to let go of the good, so that it can reappear again in relationships to come.

Exercise

First make a list of any bad feelings or situations about the relationship you are holding on to, if any.

Next make a list of the good things you are still holding on to about your ex-partner.

Put these in the hands of your 'Higher Self' (see WAY 37) to let go of (unless you have found another more effective or favourite method, in which case use it).

Choose to trust and move forward with a new and willing openness.

WAY 27 The Lesson of a Relationship

Every relationship has a crucial lesson to impart. Long-term relationships may contain a number of lessons. Learning the lesson leads to increased levels of love, confidence, understanding, self-worth and wisdom. Not learning the lesson can lead to painful experiences and feelings of valuelessness. Some lessons are so powerful that to fail at them would be similar to failing a shamanic or mastery-level test, leading to heartbreak, tragedy, crushing failure or feeling as if we were trapped in hell.

Every lesson we seek to learn in a relationship is a lesson of maturity and love. A dark lesson, such as 'the opposite sex cannot be trusted', is in truth an unlearned or only partially learned lesson.

The lessons we do not learn in our early relationships with parents and siblings, and subsequent relationships, show up again and again until they are learned. If we have not learned a lesson we have faced time after time, it has a way of turning into a trial. Some of the trials we have gone through in our lives were merely lessons that became chronic, because they were not learned.

Many of the unlearned lessons in past relationships will be completed in the letting-go process. As we give ourselves to letting go, the lessons that are finally completed will help us be open and happy in the present.

Exercise

What was the main lesson you were looking to learn in this relationship?

On the scale of 100, at what level would you say you learned it?

What were the other lessons you were looking to learn in this relationship? To what degree or at what level would you say you learned them?

Knowing what you know now, how would you have done it differently to learn these lessons?

What was the gift (see page 194) you came to give your ex-partner? Imagine yourself opening your heart and mind at a whole new level and see yourself pouring out this gift to them.

WAY 28 Role-Playing

Role-playing is a way of gaining understanding and, through that, a release from need, pain and fear. It can be used successfully to create the benefits of moving forward. This can be done with anyone with whom you have unfinished business, as understanding brings with it the power to release.

The first aspect is to get a friend, or someone else, to help you out. This process can be done over the phone, but it is more effective in person. If this is not going to be done with someone else, you might find it useful to tape (audio or video) your exercise and experience.

Exercise

The first part begins with a closed-eye process on your own. Think of the time when you had the biggest misunderstanding with the other person involved. Imagine you are them as they were back then. Try to experience what it feels like to have their body, with all its sensations. When this feels complete, imagine what it feels like to have their emotions. What are they feeling? Experience all of the sensations. When this feels complete, sense what it is like to have their thought processes. What are they thinking about? What is it that is always on their mind? Experience the sensation of that. After you

*have completed this exercise, write down any insights
you have about what it was like being them, and why
they behaved in the way that they did.*

*For the next part of this exercise, you will once again
become the other person and let your friend question you
about anything you do not understand about what your
ex-partner did or why. If you do not have someone to
assist you with this exercise, you can do it yourself. But,
first, once again put yourself into your ex-partner's body,
and try to establish and experience what your ex-partner
was feeling. If you are doing it yourself, ask what could
have caused them to behave the way that they did. Ask
yourself how long they had been feeling the feelings they
were feeling, and even where those feelings had their
beginning.*

*Now, let your friend be your ex-partner. Ask them to
hear, feel, see and sense the way life and the relationship
was for them as your partner. Ask them to feel intuitively
what your ex-partner was experiencing in the situation
that made them act the way they did. The person
assisting you is not just to act and talk as they did; they
are to feel and describe what was going on – role-playing
as the ex-partner – describing how your ex-partner was
feeling in that situation.*

The Truth

In studying the dynamics of healing principles, I discovered a number of interesting aspects. One was that the dynamics of truth, commitment, freedom and ease are basically the same in their healing effects. Another was that all of them lead to partnership. When Jesus said, 'The truth shall set you free', he was stating the natural connection between these two healing principles: truth and freedom. Likewise there is a connection between truth and ease; the extent of the truth is the extent to which things go easily. Given the results of some of our relationships, either the relationship was not true, or the way in which we lived it was not. Given the principle of truth, difficulty in the letting-go process is simply not the truth. In other words, difficulty indicates that you are not going about it in a genuine way, that you are not really committed to letting go.

In truth, letting go can be one of the easiest healing methods there is: we simply stop holding on. When this occurs the letting-go brings about a flow of poignancy; in other words, our hearts open and there is an overwhelming feeling of tenderness and even hope.

Having truth in our lives gives us a sense of direction and puts things into their natural perspective. Holding on gives us pain – or gives us attachment, which is future pain. Truth also brings us the freedom we have been missing. Truth is not lonely. It is what leads to partnership. It allows us to give ourselves and to receive from others. If we go through a painful break-up, it may be a signal that we have not been true to ourselves or to our lives in some way. Otherwise, we would not experience this kind of pain. Emotional pain is really just a way of letting us know when something is not the ultimate truth. This pain also speaks of self-deception, of areas where we mistook our attachment for love. Any attachment is a form of self-deception. It is the thought that something outside us can make us happy. But the truth frees us, just as letting go leads us towards the truth. Pain is just a way of knowing there is still some way to go, still a lesson to be learned for the truth to be known.

Exercise

Today, keep asking for the truth to be given to you. What is the truth for your life right now? Are you acting in a truthful way?

Examine a significant relationship for areas of dishonesty and self-deception. If it is or was dishonest, it typically reflects areas of self-deception in yourself. Let go of anything you still may be holding on to in this regard.

Would you consider that your current situation represents the truth for you? If not, how do you want to change?

Ask for the truth to be shown to you today. Listen

for the truth. Feel and sense what the truth is today. If you ask for the truth today, anything can be its vehicle, such as a comment or a viewpoint from someone else, something from a book, a TV programme, a thought, a dream or a symbol. Just ask for the truth and ask that when it comes you will recognise it as your message. Be aware today and the truth shall set you free!

WAY 30   No One Can Deprive Us but Ourselves

When we refuse to let go we become depressed. This depression can last a short time or the rest of our lives. It directly affects our health and can even bring our lives to an end. The World Health Organisation has now defined depression as the number-one health problem in the world. Depression most commonly results when there has been a significant loss, especially when someone we love dies. As we mourn the loss we come fully back to life. Depression contains the fear that even if we fully return to life, it will be to face yet another loss, so we might as well stay in this depression. If we refuse to mourn or let go, we can live the rest of our life in tantrum because we feel that we have been deprived of something that we want.

Yet we cannot be deprived of anything without having chosen it. In spite of our protests to the contrary, we have ultimately made some choices to give up a person or a situation. For some reason, we did not value a person fully, we were out to prove something, or we wished to get revenge on someone else significant to us. We may have let someone leave for 'their own good', regardless of our own feelings, or we may have felt we were 'bad' for them, or that they were suffering too much. These are only some of the many reasons we might choose to let someone go, or why we chose to engineer a break-up. We may not have felt worthy of them, we may have valued something more than we valued them, or somehow we may have valued our sacrifice or some other form of paying off guilt more than keeping them. There may also have been some fear about a deeper intimacy or commitment that led us to let go of them, or some fear about losing independence, control or freedom. It may be one or all of these reasons, or even more.

As we become aware of our hidden agendas, we will discover things and issues about which we feel we have to be right; we will see beliefs that we are trying to prove true. It obviously points to a conflict because the part of our minds with which we most identify now is feeling loss, sometimes major loss to the extent of refusing to go on with life, while the other part made the choice actually to give up the partner. One way to begin to free ourselves from this sense of being victimised by life is to become aware of our hidden agendas, the sides we continue to deny. If we become aware of what we were trying to get by having a loss occur, then we could make another choice, or we could integrate the two conflicting sides into a new whole. This moves us forward.

By creating a situation that would lead to loss, we were trying to get some need met and now, by holding on, we are continuing to attempt to get a need met. It may be the same or different needs in conflict, but if we are feeling any sort of unresolved loss, we are in conflict about what has occurred. The two biggest conflicts that ultimately create feelings of loss in childhood are the mistaken need for independence and the guilt about stealing a parent's attention. We can carry these unresolved patterns into adult patterns of loss, which resurface as the need to be independent, or as guilt about competition winning, sex or intimacy.

It is here that awareness of our choices becomes important. If we choose not to deceive ourselves or not to repress some of our choices and the reasons for them, almost immediately we can learn to integrate all the warring parts of our mind and conflicting desires, and to correct choices that could only lead to pain.

Exercise

While at least part of you did not want this loss to occur, let's pretend that another part of you did want it to happen. If you are willing to pretend, all kinds of things may surface that had been hidden.

So pretend you wanted this loss to happen:

Why?

What could you possibly have been thinking that would make you want this to happen?

What is the one part of this loss that you think is for the better?

As you find these thoughts that you were hiding from yourself, you may even begin to feel as if they are coming from someone else. You may have hidden or dissociated these thoughts so well that you were totally unaware of them. As you become aware of these hidden choices, you may want to make new choices with your conscious mind and this will allow you to move forward.

WAY 31   Changing Life Patterns

We all have patterns in our lives – patterns of either success or failure. Let us begin to examine these patterns in our relationships, for they can be extrapolated to represent other patterns in our lives.

First of all, we can focus on what our lives have been like: what do we think or say to others about our relationships? From the roots of our traumatic and often repressed experiences, we have patterns that branch up and out like trees. Have you ever asked yourself why your relationships never seem to work out? Or why there is never any fire in your sex life, no matter who your partner is? Or why you are always abandoned? Or why certain things always seem to happen to you?

Our life patterns show us aspects of both our conscious and our subconscious mind. But remember: our patterns are there for a reason. They are there to protect us from our fear of losing what we have, from our fear of the unknown, to block gifts and abilities of which we are frightened, to serve as a defence over deeper pain and patterns and, finally, to keep our self-conspiracies in place. Our self-conspiracies are there to prevent us from knowing ourselves and our greatness, and to keep us from our purpose. For all of these reasons, a self-defeating pattern is not genuine. It can be removed. The more courage

you can find to face the next step, the easier it is.
Yet, ironically, it seems that we are more frightened
of the good stuff than of the negative. That may
sound peculiar, but underneath everything, many
of us have deep-rooted fears of having it all, of
having happiness, even though we believe, on the
surface, that this is what we are hoping to achieve.

In terms of the blocks (I call them 'The Great
Fears' to the 'Vision' area of the mind), the fear of
success appears to be even stronger than the fear of
failure. In longer workshops, when we get down to
core life dynamics, the fear of having it all, or the
fear of God or of happiness, emerges as the most
primordial.

Today is a good day to choose that the past and
their patterns no longer rule you.

Exercise

*Make a list of the beliefs and patterns you notice in this
break-up and/or in your relationships. For example:*

Relationships never work out.

All men are . . .

All women are . . .

Sex is only . . .

I am always abandoned.

*For each belief you no longer wish to keep, which
allows it to support a self-defeating pattern, say: 'This
belief is not the truth. This belief reflects a goal which
is keeping me from my purpose. What I now choose to
believe is . . .'*

Pretend you wanted that pattern. Why do you want

it? What purpose does it serve? When you have it, what don't you have to face that is so frightening to you? What does it prove? On whom is this pattern getting revenge? Of what gift are you afraid?

There is a natural mourning period that we all go through after the loss of anyone or anything. Yet we can also make this as short or long as we choose. We can decide how long we want the mourning to be. Holding on is a form of tantrum of not wanting to deal with reality as it is, and not wanting to let go of the past.

What is tantrum? It's a choice in which we complain, withdraw, react or hurt ourselves when life does not come about as we consciously want or expect. It can show itself as any form of failure, immaturity or lack of success.

If we are holding onto someone we were dating who left us, we obsess over events of the past, trying to figure out where we went wrong, yet dreading the answers. We work to convince our friends about how good we were, how bad or incomprehensible our ex-partners were to act as they did, how we deserve another chance, or the many scenarios that the ending of a relationship can take. Yet all of these scenarios have one thing in common – a desire to reverse time and have it all back again the way it was; a refusal to accept things as they are. Sometimes we accept the relationship ending; we just want another couple of weeks to be together so that we feel ready to move on. Sometimes we are just pissed off that they broke up with us before we had a chance to break up with them. Or at the very least we want some time to go over and over the relationship, savouring its ups and downs before we are ready to go on.

This type of 'holding-on' is a form of tantrum about someone that a part of our minds wanted to lose while other parts did not. This split, of course, set up a conflict. Every holding-on represents such a conflict. The part of our minds that is foremost is the part that now misses and wants the relationship. The fact that a part of us wanted the relationship to end does not make it any easier for us to let go of the relationship, or reduce the pain of the loss, unless we become fully conscious of the hidden part. If we uncover and integrate that part that wanted to let go with the one or ones holding on, we reach a new level of trust and confidence and take big step forward in our lives.

Often we do not want to know that part of our mind that wanted things to end and refuse to even consider that there is such a part. There may be hidden justifications, such as thinking at some level that we were doing it for their own good or doing it so as not to hurt them. This usually means that we feel we have to go in a different direction from them, or we felt they were holding us back, or that we could not have them and do or have something else too. The result is that we become irrationally annoyed that something has been taken from us, even if what was lost was the result of our own doing. These are heartbreaking situations that can turn to anger: 'How does life, or God, get away with taking something I felt I wasn't through with yet?!' However much this loss seems to hurt or depress us, it won't prove how much we loved someone; it simply illustrates how attached we were. The longer our holding-on continues, the more it turns into a tantrum. Life is waiting for us, but we refuse to play. We have taken our ball and gone home because the game is not going our way. Life may go on, but not with us. We are in protest. We are depressed. We quit. *So there!*

We can only begin to think of moving on in life when we realise that our attitudes and our ways of dealing with things will not work, and that the commiseration we get will not make us happy or satisfy us. Our tantrum will not make us happy and neither will holding on. Once we recognise that nothing will help us until we begin letting go, we can finally begin to move forward.

Being in a tantrum is the last thing we want to recognise about ourselves. It can show up in all kinds of ways, such as anger, heartbreak, depression, hysteria, withdrawal, failure, illness, even self-doubt and much more. Yet it is only when we become honest with ourselves that our lives will begin to work again. There are three ways to confirm that we are suffering from a big case of tantrum, and these can be assessed by our response to this chapter. What are you feeling as you read the chapter? The three responses that point to tantrum include: becoming more and more upset as you read this chapter. Another is denial, being absolutely sure this has nothing to do with you, and that you have never done anything like this. Or, finally, there is a feeling of horror or judgement that you or anyone else could have done something like this. This is a sure sign that we are hiding a tantrum under a compensation, although we feel we would rather die than do such a thing.

Exercise

Today is a day to do some serious evaluation of yourself and your style. Take a playful attitude to these questions and your answers.

What kind of tantrums did you have as a child?

What kind of tantrums do you have as an adult?

What kind of tantrums are you having now? Are they more attack, withdrawal or bits of both?

Do you feel justified in your tantrums or anger because of your stress or other aspects of your situation?

Is your tantrum working?

Does it make you happy?

Would you like to make another choice and take a big step toward letting go, maturity and success?

Tantrums are completely self-demeaning and self-defeating. Today, we can take a big step forward in our lives if we give up this thoroughly unattractive quality that is an attempt to control others and life. Today, make a new choice. Ask your higher mind for a new way to respond that will lead you forward to another chapter in your life.

WAY 33 Letting Go of Guilt

Whenever we withdraw, whenever we feel emotional pain of any kind, and whenever we feel bad, there is an accompanying feeling of guilt. Guilt is, in general, feeling bad about the past. This bad 'feeling' of the past suggests that the future will be the same. Thus fear, which is trying to live in the future, comes out of the unmourned past, the unfinished business of the past. Guilt is a mistake turned into a monument. It keeps us nailed to the past, rather than learning its lessons and moving forward. Guilt is a trap that keeps us punishing ourselves. 'Don't bother punishing me, God, I'm doing it myself!' Having punished ourselves or having created loss and punishment to pay off our guilt, we then feel bad/guilty about being victimised, and the cycle continues. At the bottom line, guilt is a psychologically destructive trap that we use to avoid facing the next step. Guilt is not the ultimate truth. All that is true about guilt is that we experience it and have layer upon layer of it buried within us. When a situation is fully understood, guilt disappears.

Regretting and feeling bad about what happened in our relationships is a way of holding on. Any unfinished business in the relationship, any sadness or anger, or any other emotions, go hand in hand with guilt. Guilt is a form of arrogance, a dark glamour that exaggerates our importance, keeps us stuck, and denies the responsibility (or response-ability) of every co-created event. We are all doing the best we can, given inner and outer pressures, and yet, paradoxically, we can all do better. We have all made big mistakes in what we thought was best. 'Unearthing' through feelings is what ultimately corrects guilt, by allowing us the possibility of a new level of understanding that frees us from the vicious cycle of loss, need and fear.

Guilt from past losses sets up present losses and self-destructive patterns. These are the psychological patterns that we carry from childhood. Forgiving ourselves, and letting go of the guilt, is one way of freeing ourselves from these patterns that promote failure, sacrifice and valuelessness. Our guilt keeps us withdrawn and unattractive, and punishes everyone we love by our absence.

Exercise

Outline three events from the past about which you still feel guilty. Ask yourself how you are punishing yourself for this guilt.

Now ask yourself what you feel bad, guilty or a failure about in terms of your last relationship. Ask how you are punishing yourself for these feelings.

Ask to see the truth of your own and everyone else's innocence. Let go of the guilt. You can do this on your own. Ask your higher mind to let go of any remaining guilt, thus bringing you understanding and peace in its place.

WAY 34 Reviewing the Nature of Revenge

Revenge does not work. It is an attempt to get back at another for what we think they have done to us. Revenge can be an active attack against someone else, or it can be a form of hurting ourselves to get back at them. Actually, any problem, such as illness, failure or accident contains core aspects of revenge, either consciously or subconsciously. But revenge does not work. If we 'live by the sword', we 'die by the sword'. While revenge is an attempt to make up for or defend against the original hurt, it does not satisfy us. The glee revenge brings is small compensation for our hurt, and it reinforces the pattern, so that we are left being the victim or the victimiser.

As soon as we move into the subconscious mind, we find other principles that belie the need for revenge. The first one is this: no one can do anything to you that you are not already doing to yourself. So, if you feel someone is breaking your heart, you were already breaking your own heart. If you feel they abused you, you were also already abusing yourself. Interestingly enough, when this subconscious piece is healed with yourself, it becomes easy to forgive and let go of painful situations.

Revenge misses the point. It makes life about

some problem rather than about ourselves. At this point, growth, healing and happiness stop. Happiness is the best revenge, because it is *no* revenge. We could not be happy if there was revenge. The best we can get out of revenge is a self-righteous glee. Hurting ourselves to get back at others is actually a form of masochism. Revenge is fear under the guise of aggression, the fear to live our life and to be free. While happiness is the by-product of love, intimacy and joining, revenge is a form of attack which separates further and avoids the real issue.

Revenge is an extreme form of holding on. It is a continuation of the power struggle that actually led to the break-up. A lost relationship typically reflects the 'I'll hurt myself to get back at you', or victim-type revenge. This is based on frustrated needs rather than love. It is not only a revenge on our ex-partner, but probably on one or both of our parents for not loving us more, and, of course, on God.

Psychologically, every interpersonal conflict reflects the conflict in our own mind. Revenge is the ultimate manifestation of cutting off our nose to spite our face.

Exercise

Your revenge is not getting you what you want, just as your relationship did not give you what you wanted, or you would not have lost it, despite your conscious protests to the contrary. If you are in pain, you are getting revenge. Otherwise, there is simply poignancy, as you feel and let go of any feelings that aren't happy.

Today be willing to let go of your revenge and your categorical need for revenge, realising that revenge may achieve what you think you want, but it will never succeed in taking away your hurt or your loss, or in making you happy.

If you let go of your revenge around heartbreaks and losses, you will find a gift waiting for you. The most typical gift in this regard is the gift of true love.

WAY 35   The Gift You Came to Give

When you are mourning, or when you can still
remember a problem from any relationship, it means
that there is still unfinished business in that relationship. One quick way to complete the relationship
and to move forward to a whole new level in that
relationship, or into a letting-go period, is to give
the gift or gifts that you came to give to free your
partner from pain and traps.

Once again, gift-giving is not an open invitation
to ring or even write to your ex-partner. If you have
successfully let go, you can be confident that he or
she will contact you. Contacting your ex-partner is,
ultimately, self-deception, even if your reasons for
doing so appear, on the surface, to be selfless. If you
haven't let go of the relationship, you will be 'giving'
in order to 'take', which will cause your ex-partner
to become increasingly independent. Completing
the relationship can be done in the easiest way
by gift-giving, which ties up everything that has
been left undone. When your relationship has been
completed, it will no longer matter to you if they
contact you or not.

If your pain revolves around a relationship with
someone who has died, you can still offer the gift,
releasing them from the pattern of the problem. If
your problem involves your parents or someone from

the past, as you re-imagine the problem situations and give the gifts you have to give to release and redeem them, the whole situation changes, sometimes completely, and sometimes layer by layer as new gifts are given. When you have given your gifts, you can receive the gifts that they have for you and also receive the gifts heaven wants to pass through them to you. This has the effect of changing your story about what happened and your perception of the event, releasing you from pain, loss and guilt. We can give gifts in present situations and we can go back to the negative scenes that we drag around with us from the past. This will change our whole perception of the past, giving us a new more successful script and a more confident outlook.

Exercise

Think of your present or last relationship. Think of your parents and any significant relationships you have had, especially those in which you felt victimised. Ask yourself: What was the gift you came to give them to help them, even to save them? What was the lesson you had come to help them learn? What was it you had promised to give them that would save them from themselves?

The answers that come to you will reveal gifts that you feel you have not given. But these gifts are within you, behind the doors in your mind, waiting for you to recognise, open the doors, accept the gift and share it.

Imagine yourself going to these doors in your mind, opening them, and embracing the gift. Now imagine yourself going up to this person, and giving them the gift or gifts, heart to heart and mind to mind.

Ask yourself what heaven wanted to pass through you for them? Receive that and pass it on.

Now see yourself in the same way – receiving gifts and lessons that they have for you. Enjoy the sweetness of this. Now ask yourself what heaven wanted to pass through them for you. Receive that.

Tomorrow, if you seem to be still holding on, repeat this exercise, as there may be more to give and receive. This will move you through whole layers of attachment.

On the following day, if the pain is much worse or better, you are making progress. Repeat the exercise until there is only gratitude. If it goes on for more than two days, it suggests that this relationship or situation was karmic. By 'karmic' I mean that there are different patterns at root here: perhaps soul patterns, or layers to heal that come from past generations or even lifetimes. Just continue on with this exercise each day until you feel blessed from the past and free.

If there is no change either way in three days, it means there is a level of recalcitrance, and you are just using others, or a relationship, as an excuse to not move forward. You might want to reconsider this position, as it will become increasingly painful and depressing. The gifts within you heal yourself and others, make your life easy and happy and are a big gift to all those around you.

WAY 36 Smiling Their Smile – the Gift of the Relationship

Every relationship that reaches its potential has one major gift for those who are a part of it. And there are also plenty of other gifts. Sometimes, we receive something from a partner or another that is so sweet and so deep it changes our lives forever. The love they gave us made a difference to who we are as people. Sometimes it just seems too hard to let a partner go, even though they have already left. Yet, it is only when we fully let go that we can receive the final gift of the relationship. Doing this empowers us to pass on to others what we were given. Paradoxically, it is only when we let go that we are able to receive and fully integrate into ourselves the gift that we were given. What this means on an experiential level is that the emptiness they filled by being there is now filled by our own beingness, or sense of happiness, through letting go. The gift they gave us is now ours, and the loneliness is gone. It is a part of them that was extended to us, and it has now become a part of us. It was something we learned in receiving from them. Now we can give it and make the same difference to the lives of others. Now we can experience the joy of giving as we enjoyed the delight of receiving. Sometimes, we will smile their smile out at the world, or see through their eyes, as we perceive the beauty of something. And, as this new range of life they gave us is passed on, we will feel them and the bond they have with us, no matter what our external relationship with them. We will look out at life and we will actually find ourselves, smile their smiles and we will feel happy and complete and feel the goodness and the warmth once again. Our appreciation will be natural. There is a flow that will come to both our lives as we experience the goodness they gave us, especially when we now have this gift to give ourselves.

Exercise

Today, have the courage to let someone go. Notice that there are those around you who need the same gift that was given to you. You can give it. You can make a difference in their lives. And as you do, both of you will be helped. You have the choice of being held back, or you can make a difference to those around you. Sometimes, you will make as big a difference to someone else's life as that same gift made to yours. Do you want to help? If you do, you will naturally hear the cries for help. Is your withdrawal, your holding-on, your pain, more important than helping another? Would you continue in this holding on, this indulgence, if you knew someone's life depended on your giving? You can make all the difference to someone else's life, and to your own, if you choose to give the gift.

This is a leadership principle. Whenever you are in pain, there is someone in greater need. If you give through your pain, not only the other person, but you, too, will be helped.

WAY 37 Letting Go and Your Higher Self

I am a Doctor of Psychology, a kind of artist-scientist of the human mind, with a specific interest in healing. I have seen too much, in and out of therapeutic settings, to discount a higher power, or whatever name you prefer to give it. There is also a power in the human mind that is capable of magic and miracles. I am dedicated to learning and utilising this part of our mind. Call it what you will – the higher power, the creative self, the Christ self, the Buddha self, the higher mind or the Holy Spirit – it will not be diminished. It is the part of your mind that has all of the answers you need, and it is trying to make your life easy. If you do not believe any of this, you can, of course, rely on less spiritual aids, such as psychology. However, the best and fastest way to move forward in life is always with 'grace'.

In my three decades as an explorer of the human mind, I have discovered a number of things. One is that life is only difficult when we try to do everything ourselves. This is a common malady of independent people. Interdependent people work with others and with grace a great deal more. Not that there are not problems for everyone, but interdependent people quickly remember not to try to do everything themselves. We only do this when we are trying to prove something. Interdependent people are entwined in a healthy fashion with others and with the higher self. They are better at relationships and at receiving. Every attachment that we are able to release leads us closer to interdependence and re-connection or bonding. All pain comes from attachment; all fear is ultimately a fear of loss. The more that we are able to connect with the higher self, the better able we are to live a life of ease and grace, knowing how much more satisfying and successful it is to be creative rather than attached.

The job of our higher self is to solve problems for us, to provide us with answers and to help us out of seemingly impossible situations. Mostly, we want to do it ourselves, using our everyday mind. This means that we are 'in control', even if it is miserable. And it is worthwhile to have this control, isn't it? Well, isn't it?

Letting go can be easy. We can put it in the hands of our higher self. Holding on is really only a way of hiding from ourselves, which is to say from our higher self. Who are you really? And what did you come here to accomplish? What was it you promised before you came here? What did you want to contribute? Holding on is a trap whose purpose is to delay you as long as possible. And, if you waste time, time wastes you. Do not waste yourself any longer! It is not worth it. It is time to begin again. Yes!

Exercise

Place whoever it is that you need to let go in the hands of your higher self. You might visualise, feel or sense this letting-go. You might make it a prayer, or just hear yourself saying the words. When this happens, there is usually a sense of peace, or of a gift being given in return. Make it easy on yourself, give it to your higher self.

Now place your future in the hands of your higher self. Today, place any fear, care, worry, depression, guilt or bad feeling in the hands of your higher self. You can do this by feeling or sensing, or even visualising this happening.

WAY 38   The Fire of Sacrifice

While every sacrifice is a place of inauthenticity, a place of not receiving for fear of intimacy, success, change and birth to a new level, there are times in our lives when we present ourselves with a very painful circumstance or seemingly tragic situations. The purpose of this circumstance is to reach a whole new level of consciousness and birth. This is called the 'Fire of Sacrifice'. It is a chance to advance spiritually by letting go of attachments. At a soul level we have a new level or way of life to graduate to. If we do not understand that this awareness is an opportunity to advance to the new level of joy and creativity, we can feel as if our life has ended.

The new birth is achieved by letting go of every attachment and by welcoming a new beginning as if it were already accomplished. When that which was lost − such as heartbreak, or even death − is freely given back to life, the loss is no longer experienced as a sacrifice, and a new life is about to begin. In other words, if you are willing to give someone back, you will no longer use that partner to hold you back.

To have reached this place, we will most likely have to let go of the person, the relationship we had together, our life as it was, and our dreams for how it could have been. Having done this, we can see and feel in a higher place of consciousness, and we are more open to life and grace. We are ready to embrace this new chapter in our lives, thankful for what was and thankful for what is.

Exercise

Today, take a new attitude towards pain. Use the mourning – letting go process – as one that heals, raises up, blesses, frees and begins life anew. Your choice and willingness allows present and past pain to be moved through, naturally, easily and quickly, so you can evolve. While you are in the labour of letting go, make the choice to move as gracefully as possible, so that what seemed like the end of your life will only be the end of a chapter, and the movement to a higher, better chapter of love, life and joy. Is this going to be the end of your life, or your last chapter? You can deliberately make another choice to write a new chapter and to begin again.

WAY 39 The Attachment to Taking

Taking is a key element in attachment. When we are loving, all we want to do is join and bond with others. When we have bonding, there is no sense of sadness or loss when we let go, but a poignancy, tenderness or sweet sorrow as we go on to a new chapter in our lives. Most of our relationships are combinations of love, sharing, giving, helping, friendship, tenderness, learning, healing and bonding, and on the other side they also contain boredom, attachments, fusion (see page 194), sacrifice, needs, judgement, attack, righteousness, defensiveness, power struggles, deadness, using and other forms of taking.

When we attempt to use or take from someone, even under the guise of giving, we will be pushed away, and ultimately rejected. The extent of our attachment will be the extent of our pain and holding on after the relationship is gone. It is also the extent to which we were trying to take in order to get our needs met. So, we were using them in an untrue way before the relationship ended, and now that the relationship is over, we are again using them in an untrue way to hold ourselves back. This is not a happy thought, because if we just cover it over and try to move on, our next relationship will reflect this taking, either by us taking from them, them taking from us or both trying to take from each other. We might as well heal this bit of us now. It is just a mistaken choice about how to deal with our needs. If we courageously face this now, it will save us a lot of pain. This taking, which sees our needs as an excuse to act in any way we can to attempt to meet these needs, puts us into a self-defeating cycle.

Our attachments in these relationships actually represent past attachments that we brought into the relationship – old heartbreaks from the past or lost bonding from previous relationships and childhood. It all represents our needs surfacing once more in the hope that this time they might be met.

Taking is one of the most unsuccessful things we can do. It means we are going in the wrong direction. Taking involves protecting our needs, which momentarily satisfies them, but actually reinforces them, making them stronger. In the same way, the more someone steals (both literally and figuratively), the more hungry and empty they become. None of us wants to consider ourselves to be a 'taker', but if a relationship does not work out and you have been left or wounded in some way, you can bank on the fact that you were trying to take or use, probably under the guise of giving. This is a hard thing for us to recognise or deal with, because so much denial exists around the concept or even 'label' of taking. Taking leaves us feeling needy, and we think that this feeling and urgency are a sign of love rather than a sign of how much we want to use others. Once we recognise this 'taking' as our nemesis, we are well on the way to correcting it. Otherwise, people will start to avoid and fail to respond to us, keeping as much distance as they can. You can apply this theory both during and following a relationship. If you are avoided, or when someone claims to 'need space', it is undoubtedly because you are trying to get or take something, if not overtly then energetically.

Our taking can become so chronic that we become emotional 'vampires'. If it becomes even worse, we become emotionally toxic, poisoning people and situations around us with our attitudes and the negative energy we create by taking. If we have someone like this around us, it lets us know that we have this self-hatred inside that we have buried below the level of our awareness. If we have this aspect inside us we have probably hidden it under a compensation of sacrifice. We will also feel in sacrifice to the person acting out our projection. So, therefore, we are literally creating both the actions of others, and our reactions to them.

Giving up our taking patterns leads us towards maturity, success, a loving relationship and happiness. Failing to rectify this pattern leads us in an even greater cycle of defeat, loss, pain and failure.

It's also important to consider the concept of the shadow figure. A shadow figure represents an aspect of self-hatred that we have denied and repressed. It is a fracture, in that it is something that we buried away when it caused us pain or trauma, but it is much more profound than just the pain, fear and guilt of such fractures because it also carries self-hatred. A shadow figure is a personality that we have buried because we despise it – an identifiable personality, and normally the opposite of the person we appear to be on the surface.

For example, we may have done something as children that we believe caused our parents great pain or loss. We identified ourselves as being the cause which is typical for children. For example, we may have blamed ourselves for their ill-health, relationship problems, divorce, general unhappiness or even death. Instead of living with the great guilt of being a bad and wicked person, we labelled that part of ourselves as being bad, and repressed it away. But it exists within us as a shadow figure, and it festers there as it is left to wallow in the belief that it is bad. A shadow figure hides a belief that we are bad or wicked. This self-concept may at times cause us to act in such a way but it is not the ultimate truth. Whatever we might have believed at the time to cause us to shut it away, it was just part of a conspiracy to hide our true goodness, power and purpose. The important thing to realise here is that we simply perceived this part of ourselves to be bad, and it was this mistaken perception that caused the shadows. We need to go back to the original trauma or heartbreak and uncover the reasons why we blamed ourselves, why we felt rejected, or why we believed that we were wicked or evil. With this awareness, we can forgive ourselves and see that we are all truly good no matter what may have gone wrong. Punishing ourselves for guilt and turning our self-hatred into shadow figures is one of the major reasons that bad things happen to good people.

Exercise

Examine your present relationship or lost relationships. Examine relationships with your friends and acquaintances. Where do you feel unsuccessful, or that you were being avoided? What was it you were trying to take from them? How were you trying to use them? Your honesty now can be a big part in ending the self-deception that accompanies your heartbreak, holding-on or attachment.

Make a new choice to give. Remember, mouthing the words will mean nothing if you do not intend to fulfil them. The acid test of whether you are trying to take or not, is whether or not someone moves away from or towards you.

Ask yourself how many shadow figures you have hidden inside you, of the 'taker', the 'user', the 'vampire' and the 'toxic person'. These shadows are a mistake that can be easily corrected if you wish. Give these to your higher mind to integrate for you. You will now be able to use all of their energy in a positive way.

The Script Assigned – Rules for Relationship

People live by rules, or recipes, for certain situations. These are rules we have made for ourselves and rules that were imposed upon us. We live by rules unless we have reached a high enough awareness to turn our rules into principles. Rules are defences, decisions that have come out of painful situations. They are designed to prevent us from being hurt. The only problem is that rules are meant to be broken. Psychologically, defences attract attack and bring about the very thing they are trying to prevent. Rules are old, largely because they are static and inflexible and don't respond to the situation as it is – only as some painful situation was. The unresolved pain under every rule begs to be let out. The bigger the rule, the more the pain hidden beneath it, and the bigger the pain that will be called towards it to reopen the defence and allow the unfinished business to be finished.

We get upset in relationships because someone has broken our rules. Many times we do not even communicate our rules but expect our partners to be mind-readers. 'If they loved us, they would know, they would do what we wanted, or they would not do what we didn't want . . .' So when an ex-partner breaks our rules, it hurts. Not only does it hurt, but in our scripts we assigned them the supporting actor or actress roles to our stardom. Even if they seem to be given a lion's portion of the plot, there is only one star and that, of course, is us. We cannot give anyone else an equal footing because it would expose us to potential loss and pain. This is a sort of defence mechanism, and we do this out of our fear of an equal partner, which is a fear of intimacy. Without healing this fear, we will never turn our rules and scripts into principles and reach partnership and co-creativity. Now is the time to finish the pain inside and turn those rules into principles.

Exercise

Make a list of the major rules you have for relationships, about fidelity, honesty, communication, etc. Ask yourself intuitively: When you made up this rule, with whom was it made and in what circumstances?

Ask your higher mind to carry you and everyone in the situation back to their centres, to that place of peace and innocence, so you all might experience peace, wholeness and grace. From this place, give the people in the situation the gifts you have come to give them. As you give the gift, receive it also into your life. What principle now comes into your life? What does your script look and feel like now?

WAY 41 Happiness Is Your Best Gift to the World

Look around you. How many happy people do you know? Those genuinely, happy, infectious and irrepressible people are a great gift to the world. They lead by example, helping others back to their centres of peace, grace and laughter. They help you realise that happiness is not dependent on some outside thing, but that it is a continuous stream from within. Their happiness is quietly 'enthusiastic', which comes from the Greek *en theos,* meaning 'in God'. It is so helpful to be able to see and feel a lived version of the goal of happiness when we see happy people. This encourages and energises us, reminding us what life can be. We recognise that happy people are a gift to us and a gift to life.

As we give happiness to the world, our own happiness is increased. And giving and receiving this happiness for ourselves increases it for the world. Anything more than momentary happiness seems to be a rare gift in life, tied for most people to the rise and fall in our fortunes, but as we radiate happiness, this gift resonates and amplifies in others. Imagine the gift you give to your partner by being happy. When a person finds that rush of spring-like happiness welling up from inside, if they don't have a love partner they are typically soon to find one.

If we have a partner when happiness strikes we will reach a new honeymoon period together. Happiness can continue throughout the relationship, in spite of its ups and downs and many lessons, because the treasure of relationships is their potential to make ourselves and others happy by joining.

Notice how a happy person in the family becomes its centre, inspiring the whole family to love and be happy, making every load lighter. Happiness is not only attractive, it is magnetic. It makes strangers feel like friends, and grievances unimportant in the true scheme of things. Happiness coming out of love only wants to love and bring happiness. Happiness received from grace carries grace to others without having to think about it, but just by being itself.

Happiness finds the lovableness in all creatures. Happiness has traded in judgement for delight. It celebrates whatever is given to it, and sees love and fun in everyone and everything. Happiness in life is equivalent to mastery in life. Your happiness blesses all life and is, in turn, blessed by it.

Exercise

Start the day by choosing happiness, sharing any little bit of it you discover to increase it. You may begin by thinking of what makes you happy or what you have to be happy about. Imagine happiness flooding into, washing over and through you, at the same time it is emerging from the very centre of your being and radiating outward. It is God's gift, received and shared.

It will make all the difference in your day. It will make all the difference in your life. It will make all the difference to the world.

WAY 42 Fantasy and Expectations – the Expectation and Holding-On Stage

Relationships can be filled with fantasy and when we are not in relationships there is even more fantasy. We dream of what we are missing both within and without relationships. We augment our partner with the help of movie stars, famous or idealised people, and infatuations. The more we fantasise, the less we want the reality of our partners to intrude upon our experience. The more we fantasise, the harder it is for our partners to satisfy us, or even for us to be satisfied at all. In the unlikely case that we do have a fantasy fulfilled, we realise that somehow that fantasy was not quite enough to satisfy us. Fantasy generates fantasy in an ever-deepening vicious cycle of need, fantasy, lack of satisfaction, more fantasy, less satisfaction, and so on.

Fantasy and expectations have the same deleterious effect on relationships. An expectation is the picture of how things or people should be; fantasy is the picture of how we want it to be. Both are hard to fulfil, and become even more elusive as the relationship goes on. When an expectation or fantasy is not met we are disappointed, but we would be disappointed even if they were fulfilled. We would still want more.

An expectation is a demand and we all hate to have demands made of us. Even if we fulfil the demand, we felt we had to do it, so instead of a reward we feel only a sense of 'having to' or sacrifice. With an expectation we either do it under duress or we rebel against doing it at all. An expectation is unsuccessful whether we lay it on ourselves or others. So we push ourselves on and on to greater and greater expectations until we fail.

Demands come from needs, which generate a sense of inadequacy. This leads us to push ourselves or fantasise rather than to venture forth. If we feel whole, confident or bonded, we do not make demands or fantasise. In an expectation, we demand that others do for us what we are not doing for ourselves or for others. The only thing that can fulfil us is giving out of choice, which lets us enjoy giving and opens to the door to receiving. Expectations, fantasy, demands and the needs that drive them, are all attempts to take without being able to receive. This is so unfulfilling that it can quickly make us even more dissatisfied and eventually drive us out of a relationship or keep us from having one altogether. Expectations and fantasies are attempts to compensate for needs, but they make us both more stressed and more needy. A sure sign of expectations or fantasies is the frustration and disappointment that results.

We all fantasise. It is only when fantasy becomes a way of life that we cheat ourselves of the opportunity to live fully and to be happy. With fantasy we try to meet needs from daydreams the same way that a starving man tries to slake hunger with fantasies about food. It does not work. If we spend a lot of time fantasising as single people, our minds can not tell the difference between an imagined lover or the experience of a real one, because it all shows as images in our mind. So if we have a fantasy image of a lover, to our mind we have no need of an actual person because the space for the lover image is filled. In spite of fantasy being based on needing something, we cannot receive it because both our fantasy and our needs block it.

All of our fantasies and expectations are fed by our needs, which is some form of attachment or holding on. When we fantasise about connecting with an imaginary person we don't feel the joining or satisfaction that comes from real connection. Our expectations demand that they be the way we think they should be to satisfy us. Fantasy and expectations are built on the vain attempt to fulfil our needs and attachments. The frustration of every need and attachment compounds the loss, pain and need that we have. All of this energy is extremely unattractive and serves to push people away from us. In other words, if we are holding on to someone, our holding-on and all of its unattractive and needy energy is the very thing that blocks our ex-partner from returning. Paradoxically, only when we let go can we disperse our self-defeating programme.

There is a particular stage of growth that we all go through where fantasy, expectations and holding on are the main issues we need to face. This occurs at our most independent stage in life, when we are most dissociated, unable to experience many of our feelings except when we are holding on. This stage of growth is a place where we compensate for our needs, fear, lost bonding and the resultant feelings of inadequacy, which all generate demands, holding on, fantasy, expectation, trying too hard, pursuing too many goals, perfectionism and giving up.

All of our compensations do not work in the long run, simply because the very nature of a compensation includes defensiveness, inability to receive, sacrifice, trying to prove something and denial of certain feelings. Also, the defences we use at this stage – such as holding on, perfectionism and demands – are particularly self-defeating in relationships or within ourselves.

While an independent person may seem a tower of strength, it is interesting to note that the extent to which they are independent is also the extent to which they are holding on to the past. It could be an old lover, or it could even be a parent or sibling, but we still light a candle for that person everyday in the chapel of our old love. This actually prevents us from having a significant partner now, because we are still holding on.

Perfectionism is another common trap we fall into at this stage. It is a compensation for lost bonding where we felt unloved. Now we feel that we would be loved if we could only do things perfectly. To a perfectionist, anything less than perfect is failure. This is self-defeating because we then feel that if we have not 'walked on water' lately, we are a failure. The busyness and demands of perfectionism are a turn-off in relationships, as is the pushing or quitting that comes from being unable to do things perfectly.

Exercise

It is time to let go of our fantasies, expectations, attachments and perfectionism. It is time to focus and set goals instead. If we have too many goals, it is time to let go of any that are not true. Commit to and complete projects that are true, and let go of the ones that are not. It is time to let go of loved ones from the past to whom we are still clinging. We are using them to avoid living our lives and having true love now. It is time to integrate the perfectionist and the unloved, inadequate one for which it compensates.

Imagine however many 'perfectionist' selves you have inside melting into however many 'inadequate', 'unloved' and 'needy' personalities you have inside. Then imagine the integrated energy melting back into you.

Now do a fantasy check. How much do you fantasise? Is it about an ex-partner or ex-partners? Is it about people with whom you work or are acquainted? Are there movie stars, or is there an ideal partner? Seriously examine how your fantasies are holding you back and let them go.

Do an expectation assessment. Whenever you hear yourself using the words 'have to', 'need to', 'got to', 'ought to', 'must' or 'should' you are putting demands on yourself. The extent to which you react to others putting demands on you shows you the demands that you are making on yourself inside because you will react or be stressed only by the demands that you already have for yourself.

Examine your attachments. What do you need? What are you holding on to? What do you need to be your way? You will be upset every time an attachment is not met. If you let your attachments go, you will feel more bonded, more adequate, more flexible and less reactive. Paradoxically, only by letting go of your attachments can you have what you want.

Today, it is time to let go of your perfectionism as a completely self-defeating action. You can set your goal to get it perfect without demanding it of yourself and driving yourself too hard. Do your best and let it go, otherwise you obsess which is always the sign of a trap.

All of these elements, if learned and healed, will help you to move out of the holding-on stage that we all have to go through. This stage is one of the very toughest stages in which to find a partner or to enjoy the one you have. The sooner you learn the lessons, let go and get past this stage, the sooner you will become more successful in life and in relationships.

WAY 43 What Is it that You Want?

This is a good time to examine what you really want from life. What do you really want in a relationship? As you have been going through this book, you have probably become more and more willing to move forward in your life. But what do you wish to move towards? How do you want your life to turn out? Do you want your life to end here, stopped by this emotional hazard? Your only joy here on this earth is to be happy, or to heal in order to be happy. Most of life is an attempt to do things to make us happy. All the rest is what we are doing to prove that we are good people. Think about it. What do you always tell your friends about your life? Usually this comes under three general categories: a) how good it is!; b) how bad/difficult it is; or c) how hard it was but I accomplished it!

These are stories we have been telling for years. They usually put a slight, or not so slight, barrier between us and our audience, because we would tell this to any audience. In other words, we are not entering into a truthful and meaningful discourse or relationship; we are not relating, we are telling our story. Good stories are compensations for feeling bad or guilty inside. Bad stories are about how tough life is: please love me (victim story) . . . or how hard/busy life is, but I have handled it (hero story), or how rotten other people are and, of course, I am so good (victim story). All of this hides how valueless we feel inside; in other words, we can't feel very good about ourselves if we are willing to punish ourselves or compensate through hard work for our bad feelings. All of these stories are part of our conspiracy against ourselves. We use them to hide who we are and to hide our major gifts (see page 194).

What do you want in your life? You are at a birthing point, a place for a new beginning, a new chapter. You can choose to live in a whole new way, and leap forward out of your present experience. You can choose a happy, peaceful story. It may be undramatic, but the love and creativity would more than satisfy the need for stimulation.

Exercise

Look at what your story is hiding. What is the gift hidden so well under your conspiracy against yourself and against your greatness? Remember that your difficulty or problem tends to be the opposite of your gift, thus keeping it well disguised. Once you have this gift in mind, use it when you think of your future. Nothing can go wrong with your life when you are employing your gift. Become aware that you have no neutral thoughts. Your thoughts are either about love and success, or against them. Every time you think an unhappy thought about the past or future, see and feel your gift added to this thought or situation. You will notice everything goes better with your gift.

Today, share this gift in whatever way you feel inspired to with someone else. As you give it, feel yourself receiving it. You will naturally feel better and more confident about life!

WAY 44 Hanging on to Bits and Pieces

After a relationship is over, we work to let it go, to free ourselves. First we let go of the negative aspects and then, usually, the positive ones. But the toughest things to release are the bits and pieces that were really great about that partner. Sometimes we hold on to very wonderful experiences that we had with them, and sometimes we hold onto bits and pieces of their body, or sometimes it is the special gifts they had, or amazing things they did or gave to us.

We collect pieces of many different relationships, like charms on a bracelet. One thing is for sure, if we hold on to all of these pieces, something as good or better than this particular quality is not given space to materialise in the present. Years or decades later, we can still pine for something we lost in a relationship or with a certain person. We use this charm bracelet and the pieces we have kept to ward us against our loneliness. We finger each bit hanging from the bracelet, savouring some sweet memory of a time gone past. As we savour the memory, we realise what we are missing and we long for the return of the person attached to the bit. We are forever ignoring the principle that we could never really have lost them if we fully valued or wanted them. Since the person with the special bit for some reason has gone, we long not so much for them but for their special bit.

Yet it is these very relics, saved as the finest parts of relationships gone past, that serve to keep these very qualities or experiences from happening once again. Only by letting go of each piece on the charm bracelet, each special part of the reliquary, can we once again open ourselves to a whole new day, where all the blessings of the past can join us with present beauty.

Exercise

Make a list of the charms on your bracelet. Choose to let go of each one and then release the charm bracelet itself. Imagine each charm put into the hands of your higher self, and then do the same with the bracelet. Make a new start. Be grateful for what was past and know that even better things are coming your way now.

WAY 45 Happiness or Self-Concepts

Happiness is a state of being that comes from giving ourselves and receiving grace, love and all good things. A self-concept is a belief that supports our ego identity, or who we think we are. These self-concepts are established as we begin to take on personality in our lives, something we all go through. As we move through the dependent stages of life into the independent stages, we build up a strong ego with many self-concepts. To continue growing to interdependence or partnership, and finally to radical or spiritual dependence, we must begin letting go of our self-concepts. Every letting go we do helps in this. We let go of self-concepts as we let go of our attachment to anyone or anything because they are a person or a thing outside with which we have identified ourselves, in a false way. Therefore, we believe that happiness comes from these self-concepts rather than the relationship itself or from what we give.

At some level all self-concepts are acquisitive and attempt to 'take' in order to be happy. This is just one of the ways that a self-concept works against happiness. After we reach the independence stage, to go forward in happiness there is both an evolution in our self-concepts and what we identify with, and

letting go of many of our self-concepts because
they are false or mistaken. This allows us to let
go of 'my way' to find 'our way'. As we continue
further, we let go of 'my' and 'our' way to find
heaven's way, which will include my and our way
more successfully. In other words our relationship
with ourselves and others becomes even happier.
This ascendancy both of the self-concepts within
us and its reflection in our relationships outside us,
occurs all through the evolution of our self-concepts
until we reach Oneness. The less we are caught in
this competition and its effects the more we can be
happy, the more we can leave 'doingness' behind
to reach our 'beingness', which directly correlates
to our happiness.

Our self-concepts can achieve the short-lived happiness that comes from achieving something, but every
self-concept within us has its own idea of what that
achievement is. This sets up a state of conflict among
our thousands of self-concepts about what happiness is and how it can be attained. A self-concept
might be a belief like: 'I'm strong', 'I'm good', 'I'm
stressed' or 'I'm a survivor', or a negative belief, such
as, 'I'm a victim' or 'I'm bad'.

Every self-concept has its own logic system and
plan to get happiness. Every self-concept thus sets
up a strategy of hard work or having to do something
that is an attempt to get, win, prove, or avoid
something. Ultimately, every self-concept is a role
or some form of sacrifice. When we feel there is too
much sacrifice, we usually try to palm off as much
as we can on to someone else. We feel that if we are

experiencing so much sacrifice, everyone else should have to sacrifice too. We do not think of ways to heal the sacrifice, only how to pass it on or to make others sacrifice as well. On the other hand, happiness does not demand anything. Happiness does not have to be worked for; it is a state of being.

Working hard or being busy are attempts to be happy that avoid or miss the relatedness, bonding and spiritual identity that naturally give us happiness. If we approach a task with bonding and grace it is easily and effectively accomplished. Conversely, our self-concepts lead us to think that keeping the status quo and avoiding change represent the recipe for happiness, so they constantly work for their own continuance, whether or not this has anything to do with our happiness. Even negative self-concepts fight for their continuance as a form of happiness. If continuance of self-concepts were the only aspect that we had to worry about, it would be difficult enough, but our situation is more complicated, because each self-concept is also interested in ascendancy. This sets up competition and power struggle within our ego and among our self-concepts. We also project and carry these conflicts into our outside relationships, so we attempt to gain domination and ascendancy over those around us. This ascendancy is manifested by a need to measure ourselves against others because of a need or in an attempt to be superior. If we can't manage this completely, we attempt to do this in some way by judging, which allows us to feel superior. The level at which we compete like this is the same level to which we invest in something that cannot make us happy. The judgement and power struggles it sets up with others generates threats and fear, which our self-concepts defend against with anger and control, to avoid defeat. This moves us as far away from the experience of happiness as we can get.

As a state of being, happiness wants to share itself in order to increase, or multiply. It needs no defence and it wants no part of the jobs that our self-concepts think up. It recognises that this only leads to competition and power struggle, which are the opposite of peace and happiness.

Let's say that as a child we acquired self-concepts of being selfish. These represent places in childhood where we lost bonding, where we might have been labelled 'selfish', while feeling that our needs had not been met, and because we had been forced, as children, to get our needs met ourselves. For this reason, we acquired the self-concept that we were selfish.

As we get older we hide or compensate for the 'selfish' self-concepts by sacrificing our wants and needs. As we get into love relationships, our selfish self-concepts often come out causing our partner's 'sacrifice' self-concepts to respond to try and handle them. Sometimes it's just the opposite; however, the more that our needy, selfish self-concepts emerge, the more our partners are thrown into their in-dependent or sacrificing self-concepts to counter or balance these. This can reach a point where part-ners finally leave us because of our needy, selfish behaviour. At times we don't even have a clue why they left, why we had become so unattractive, and what it was that drove them off.

As we grow up, we typically build a strong sense of our self and our identity. This strong sense of self sees our happiness as acquiring and depending on things outside us. As we lose these things or people, so goes our happiness. As we gain these things, at some point we realise that it is not the things or people themselves that give us happiness, but our relationships and our giving to them, which opens us to receiving and enjoying their qualities. By this time, we have built a strong identity of being hard working and busy, even if we act lazy, with 'lazy' self-concepts prominent, and our minds are busy with the effects of our self-concepts trying to work to achieve a short-lived happiness.

As we evolve from a strong sense of self, we must let go of these self-concepts and all of the roles and personalities that they generate. This relinquishes our 'doing-ness' and returns us to 'being'. There becomes less of us and more of partnership, less of us and more of creativity, less of us and more of heaven. In the final essay (see WAY 50), we realise that we don't actually have to *do* anything for happiness. We no longer require the false needs artificially generated by self-concepts to keep a certain identity going. We realise that neither the identity nor having our needs met made us happy. Working for happiness is a misconception, which sets up a vicious circle of working to ensure that our needs are met instead of simply giving and receiving. The misconception is generated by the indulgence-guilt-sacrifice cycle. It keeps us working and compensating, but unable to receive. But happiness naturally allows us to give and receive at whole new levels.

Once we have reached the independent stage of our lives, in which we have a strong sense of self, it is important to evolve to interdependence, to become more happy, successful and loving. To graduate to partnership, our self-concepts must successfully work in concert with others. This requires negotiation and a better communication about who sacrifices when, so we can maintain our self-concepts while still vying for ascendancy within the higher framework of partnership and teamwork. This requires letting go of more independent self-concepts for more inter-dependent ones. Co-operative self-concepts are more evolved self-concepts than competitive or sacrificing self-concepts.

But at this stage, we also begin to let go of self-concepts or melt them away with love, for-giveness and integration, so that we move forward in openness, equality, bonding and enjoyment. This opens us to ourselves (our own being), to other beings, and to Being, or God, which is all about love and happiness. As evolution occurs, we no longer have to work or fight to supply the needs of our self-concepts because, the more we progress, the more we realise our true identity as spirit or a child of God. So we need less and less and receive more and more. This allows us a sense of worth from our beingness and from happiness. As we go on, we move toward more of the joining that is a window for heaven and away from the separating walls of self-concepts, which keeps grace and others out.

As we let go of more self-concepts, we become less defensive, aggressive and competitive. We become more open and loving, and happy to give, receive and feel joy. Because we increase our use of our whole minds rather than filling them with self-concepts and senseless jobs, we become more creative. We are caught less in futile passions and we come to know our will, which is the power of mind and spirit focused for good. Our will is not our 'willpower', or even our power of choice, but the power of our being extending itself to bring truth and spirit. We become less of who we thought we were and more of heaven, the consciousness of Oneness.

Exercise

It is time we let go of who we think we are, and to know ourselves as we really are. Today, let go of every negative belief that you have about yourself. This will be easy to do unless you are holding on to this negative self-concept for a certain purpose.

I. Examine any area in which you are upset, defensive or aggressive. What self-concept are you defending? Why? Will it make you happy? When?

II. Invoke your higher mind today and commit to returning to the wholeness of your being, supported by Being. As you progress, your ego can become alarmed at its loss of self-concepts, which give it stability and separation. Usually at this point your ego threatens you to the extent that you feel you will die. But remember: you are not your self-concepts and only your ego will die. You will be born again in a new level of love and light.

WAY 46 Doing Your Part

My years of experience examining many minds has given me many crucial insights, and one of the most central is the following: We all have a purpose, and it is one that only we can fulfil. Metaphorically, we could say that this purpose is a promise we made to make a difference in the lives of our family and in the world. As we fulfil our purpose, we also fulfil ourselves. As we know and become our own self, and evolve towards becoming our best or higher self, we become a channel for grace. This way of being is naturally successful, and invites and assists others also to succeed naturally.

When we let go, we allow others caught in similar situations to have the grace to let go. Our release becomes a channel for grace. Our evolution clears a path for everyone around us to move forward. We are locked in a certain energetic configuration with the people closest to us. As one person in the configuration shifts forward, everyone else in the configuration is allowed to shift forward. Letting go will be one lesson our children won't have to learn the hard way. Otherwise, every unresolved lesson gets passed down to our children to learn for themselves. Learning major lessons is like clearing a minefield through which our children, and other loved ones, will have to pass. By doing our part and letting go, what is now a minefield for us can be a playground for them.

Letting go and moving forward in a timely fashion is our gift to the world. This means there is one less bit of pain and illusion to resonate with other pain. There will now be a bit more flow, which will help everything unfold more naturally. Letting go and moving forward removes one more trap of pain from the world and adds that same degree of understanding. Healing moves us towards happiness and the realisation of our wholeness. Holding on just moves us towards more pain and death. It takes courage to move forward. And, in moving forward, anything could happen, even good things.

Exercise

Today, every time you think of the future, see, feel and sense its brightness. This is a choice – a choice to change all of your thoughts of pain to those associated with feeling good. In particular, use the time just before you fall asleep, and the time just after you have awakened, to choose a happy day. See the future as brightening, feel it as free, hear yourself talking as you do when you are your best self. Notice every thought of fear, loneliness, depression, grievance or any form of bad feeling. Since every thought we have helps to create our reality, it is important that we act responsibly – not only in terms of behaviour and feelings, but also in our thoughts as well. Every time you catch yourself in anything but a happy, abundant, loving thought, make a new choice. Choose, see and feel the results of your choice as vividly as possible. Your thoughts are the orders you send into your life for that which comes to pass.

WAY 47 Happiness and the Ego's Schemes

There is the happiness that comes from love, creativity and grace, and there are the schemes of the ego to try to achieve happiness. The ego suggests all sorts of schemes, but they are ways that primarily build itself up. As strategies for happiness, they do not work and typically lead us to a good deal of pain, but we keep listening to the ego until we finally learn the lessons involved.

For instance, the ego tells us that being special will make us happy, but this only makes us feel glad or special for a short while. Then we have to guard our status jealously and woe to the person who does not treat us in the way we think we should be treated. The ego also tells us that getting our needs met will make us happy. It has lots of suggestions about how we can do this: by taking from others, being taken from, working too hard, laziness, being needy, being undependable, being sick, grabbing the limelight, hiding ourselves, getting revenge, being heartbroken, paying off guilt, indulging ourselves, sacrificing ourselves, competing, winning, being the worst, and staying separated. And those are only a few of the tricks the ego has to hand.

Primarily the ego suggests that we victimise others or become victims ourselves in an attempt to get our

needs met. This includes losing someone in relationship to get attention, sympathy, and so on. Then it
suggests holding on and trying to get past needs met
in the present, perhaps by holding onto grievances.
We then have the right, at least in our own minds,
to take and become a victimiser because of what
happened to us. This is one of the great blind spots
we have about all of the places where we have been
victimised. If we don't heal, we either withdraw,
which hurts those we love, or we feel we have a carte
blanche, a justification for current bullying or taking
behaviour because we have been wounded. Many
times after we have moved through our dependency
and victimisation we become independent to ensure
that we are never hurt again. But, as a result, we
become inadvertent victimisers. In other words if
we are victimised and don't heal, we pass it on.
We may do so in different forms, but we pass it
on. For example, someone who was heartbroken
may now seek to control others to prevent anyone
from being heartbroken. The extent to which we
heal, love, reach out, communicate and forgive, is
the extent to which this healing is also passed on.

Some of our ego schemes work to get our needs
met in the short-term, but never in the long run.
Even if our needs are met they come back, so the
schemes do not make us happy. They only built up
the ego and made us more separate, which is the
antithesis of happiness. The ego promises to get rid
of our fear, but it will only do this partially, as the ego
itself is the principle of separation, made up of fear,
guilt, pain, competition, domination, subjugation,

specialness, comparison, self-attack and belief that we are our bodies.

The alternative to listening to the ego is listening to our higher mind, which will show us the way to happiness and bring happiness through grace. Our higher mind helps us find the way out of the ego schemes that have caught us up in pain and traps, once we recognise our mistakes. It takes only willingness to be willing for it to kick in with guidance and grace. Changing towards happiness would be relatively easy if we were willing to identify with the higher mind rather than the ego. The ego tells us it will make us happy, leading us on a joyride that has death as it final goal. This is the ultimate self-attack of the ego, which wants us to identify with our bodies as ourselves, rather than with ourselves as spirit. Then it attacks us, telling us our bodies are not good enough for us. It leads us into such painful or exhausting traps, and then it suggests we die rather than change, finally feeling that it is even better than us. Having become a legend in its own mind, the ego wants to get rid of us, not realising the insanity of what it wants and somehow thinking it would survive our death.

Let's take a long look at how much we are invested in grievances, in the past, and in trying to ensure that our needs are met. Every place where we were heart-broken, or where we failed or have been victimised represents an ego scheme at work. Every time we are in pain, we will find an ego scheme at work but we won't find more than momentary success, love or happiness. We may think that our neediness or pain will encourage others to respond, but it will never truly happen, as long as the ego is in control.

Exercise

Today it is time to recognise our ego schemes, and acknowledge that they are a mistake, and that they won't make us happy. Then we can ask our higher mind for the grace and miracles to show us the way to true happiness easily. We could be a willing student, unlearning what we need to unlearn, and learning what is necessary. The ego hates change that matures and evolves us, because it is the only thing that will get us out of its schemes and into happiness. Our ego schemes attempt to make us sacrifice or have us be victims for most of the following reasons. Some of the reasons are just stronger than others at different times.

Our ego's schemes:
* *allow us to do something we want to do but haven't allowed ourselves*
* *allow us not to have to do something we don't want to do*
* *encourage us to attempt to get our needs met*
* *make us special*
* *get us attention*
* *get something for us*
* *encourage us to rebel*
* *protect us from healing some fear*
* *show we are right*
* *win, dominate or subjugate*
* *prove something*

- *attempt to save our families by roles and sacrific*
- *attempt to get revenge*
- *attempt to defeat someone*
- *attempt to attack ourselves, others or God*
- *give us an excuse*
- *hide from our power, our purpose and our identity*
- *have others take care of our needs*
- *control ourselves or others*
- *hide from gifts, opportunities or talents*
- *compete with and defeat others*
- *want us to believe we are only our bodies*
- *encourage sacrifice*
- *encourage us to become a victim or victimise others*
- *cause us to indulge ourselves*
- *cause us to feel guilt so we don't have to chang*
- *encourage us to play one-upmanship*
- *make us feel weak, inadequate and separate*
- *delay and distract us*
- *build its future continuity*
- *keep the status quo and fight change*
- *keep us independent*
- *show our superiority or inferiority*
- *block love and intimacy*
- *make us feel guilty*
- *attempt to pay off guilt*

A Chronic Holding-On Hides an Indulgence

When we keep holding on to someone or something and refuse to let go and move on, even when we know that it is not good or true for us, then we are using our holding-on to hide an indulgence to which we are attached. What is an indulgence? It could be smoking, abuse of food, alcohol or drugs, hysterical behaviour, emotional indulgence or even hanging on to an unsuitable partner, despite any pain. Our embarrassment or shame about this indulgence leads us to keep it hidden, even to the point of hiding it from ourselves, and no amount of coaxing or cajoling will influence us to let go of our partners because that is not really the issue. The chronic holding-on is itself a defence, to allow us to continue holding on to the hidden indulgence. We need to become aware that the real issue is about this indulgence. It is some small vice that makes us feel guilty and makes us want to sacrifice and compensate. Because of our sacrifice, we feel a need to refresh ourselves and feel justified in our indulgence because we 'sacrifice' so much or work so hard. This puts us into a vicious circle.

If we become aware of the indulgence and realise that it is not satisfying us, that our indulgence-sacrifice trap does not work, we can motivate ourselves to let it go so we can move forward to what will truly satisfy us.

Our indulgence is an ego strategy. The ego uses indulgence to make us feel special and then ashamed and guilty. By using this strategy the ego intends to comfort us to make up for the pain, heartbreak or loss of bonding. But the indulgence does not give us the comfort, joy or satisfaction that bonding would bring with its love and success. The ego actually uses the separation of the lost bonding, the specialness, guilt and shame to build itself and keep itself strong. Ego strategies are defences that never really work. They bring pain, dissatisfaction or the very thing we were trying to prevent with the defence. Of course, the ego is quick with another plan or defence that builds our hope, goes on for a while but also will not work. This can cause the problem to be layered and seemingly complex. In truth, this is not the case. We simply need to let go of the indulgence or to end the key separation involved through joining to re-establish the bonding. This may be with a parent or it may be with ourselves, our partner or with heaven.

Indulgence is an attempt to take, but it can not receive. It is some treat to which we give value because we think it will make up for what we lost or what has been missing since we lost some key bonding. Indulgence never fills the emotional hole we feel inside ourselves, so we just do more of it to try to satisfy ourselves. This only makes us feel more guilt, which causes us to withdraw more, and makes us less able to receive.

Indulgence glitters but it is not gold. It will cause some type of hangover or heaviness as a result. Indulgence becomes more valued than our relationships and this form of surreptitious taking erodes relationships and begins to make us more and more unhappy.

Exercise

Take a look at chronic patterns of holding on in your life. It is the area in which you are not moving forward. Dwell on what the hidden indulgence could be. Once you discover it, examine the indulgence-sacrifice circle you are in and what effect this has really had in your life. Examine how much the indulgence has really satisfied you and how happy it has made you. Examine the price you have had to pay for it.

If it has not worked, you may want to let it go along with your other ego 'strategies' that keep you holding on, so life can bring you what can really satisfy you. If you do not like that price you are paying for the indulgence, which is not really making you happy, you may want to make a new decision. Once you let go of the hidden indulgence, the chronic holding-on will naturally fall away, allowing life to show you what can really work.

Ask yourself with whom the key bonding was lost, and think about how it has caused you to hold on to this old partner? Imagine yourself now with lines of light connecting you to them.

Now go back to when that bonding was lost and once again imagine the lines of light connecting you with them.

WAY 49 Happiness, Depression and the Framing of God

We all know that depression comes from a loss from which we have not recovered. Depression is full of painful feelings, such as sadness, loss, fear, need, abandonment, hurt, heartbreak, guilt, unworthiness, exhaustion, hopelessness and futility. It is not widely appreciated that only we can make that choice for loss, when we follow another of the ego's harebrained and unsatisfying schemes. In other words, part of our mind was in on the story or script that brought about the depression and is continuing this life script as a depressing story. Now the ego's idea for depression has become another scheme to try to get something. In the end, depression is a finger of accusation pointed toward the one who left us, or someone who seemed to cause the loss. It is also a blame directed towards past loves and our parents for not having done it right. And there is self-blame involved too. However, ultimately, in the deepest parts of the mind, the depression is a finger of blame pointed towards God for failing us, for being a bad or weak God who failed to save us or make us happy.

This may seem like a difficult concept to accept, particularly for first-time readers. You may wish to come back to this way again over the years, until the message becomes clear. This concept, however, represents some 25 years of research in the deepest areas of the human mind, and whether you call the subject of our fundamental dispute God, light, spirit, or even truth, we do all carry this anger or sense of betrayal at our deepest level.

We are trying to blame and frame God for what we have done, for a plan that could never have worked to make us happy. We are attempting to blame and frame God for what we did with our ego's plan for happiness. This may sound preposterous, yet deep in the mind the ego plans to dethrone God for having failed and our ego plans to take his place. We blame God for all that we have done with the world and use this as evidence against him so we could be king of heaven. This would be ludicrous, if it were not so delusionary and painful. The ego takes our projection and misplanning as evidence that we have made mistakes and, as Nietzsche once said of the bourgeois, lives as if God were dead. This was Nietzsche's great indictment of the bourgeoisie who were living as if money were god and God did not exist. Of course, God could not have done what we accuse him of doing and still remain God. He would have lost his God licence. We, on the other hand, have all the free will we want even to the point of biting the hand that feeds us.

Our attack does not hurt God, of course, but it does hurt us, blocking our higher mind, and making it doubly hard for us to receive guidance and grace. In the final essay (see WAY 50), our death becomes our way of proving that we are more powerful than

God, because he could not stop us, and he could not follow us into death. Our ego uses this in our last-ditch attempt to be God and to prove we are right, dead right. This is one more scheme that will not make us happy. It cuts us off from grace, not because we can ever truly stop grace, but because we can turn away from it. In our ego's final competition, it competes against God, keeping this all hidden from our awareness and telling us that death is the only way out.

This is the third and most primordial layer of guilt which takes place in the deepest area of the mind. The first layer of guilt is about what we have done or failed to do. This includes anything we feel bad about, including holding on. Most people never get past this layer. The second layer of guilt revolves around our families and our attempt to save them as one of our strongest impulses. The ego hides our gifts and then suggests we try to sacrifice ourselves to save our families. In the end we use our families to hold ourselves back by sacrifice and burn-out and then by staying independent from them, because of our burn-out and failure. Even if we discover this second layer of guilt, it is one of the key conspiracies our ego uses to hold us back in life, keeping us from our gifts and our purpose. Given the state of the families in which we grew up, and their lack of bonding, we have all been caught in this one. On top of this rests the relationship conspiracy of which holding on is just a small part. The relationship conspiracy tries to give our relationships the importance of

God. It sees relationships as something powerful that has the ability to save us. It confuses special-ness, which is competitive and makes demands, with God. The relationship conspiracy can take the form of no relationships, relationships built on fighting, deadness, misunderstanding, separation within the relationship, or holding on.

This huge layer is meant to hide our family conspiracy, which contains our grievances toward our families for the pain we suffered. But this pain and our grievances merely mask our feelings of valuelessness and failure for not having saved our families from their pain, which we ended up inheriting. Within us we still have the gifts to help heal our families. The gifts are buried under the pain, sacrifice, roles, fusion, guilt, compensations, co-dependency, and dissociated independence from the past. Yet they are not hard to reach once we have an awareness of their presence. Once embraced and shared, these gifts will then help the world in amazing ways as we fulfil our purpose.

All of this still hides a deeper area or third layer of guilt, which Christians describe as 'original sin'. This is the area where we feel guilty for separating from God or oneness. We believe we have stolen God's gifts and killed him in a giant spiritual Oedipal conflict. We now feel we have a huge enemy in God and that he is angry with us. We then blame the suffering of the world on God and use it as an excuse to usurp his authority and act as if we are God. Of course we framed God, or think we did, blaming him for throwing us out of heaven, as if heaven could be a place where you are thrown out, as if anything God commanded could *ever* be disobeyed. This means that we are still in heaven, or the experience of Oneness, but we keep ourselves out of this part of our mind and into the more illusionary, dream part of our mind, the ego mind.

This attack we carry on against God, while containing our oldest most primordial guilt, is still pure misunderstanding. It is less real than the tantrum of a two-year-old against its parent. The most loving force in the universe just wants us out of the nightmare we are having about this fight, this guilt, this self-punishment and pain. If we could only focus or realise God's love for us we could forget the pain and wake up from our bad dreams. Of course, it is much easier to awaken fully from happy dreams into the joy of Oneness than from nightmares. Our holding-on and the ensuing depression has become one of our nightmares. It's time to turn this into a happy dream.

Exercise

Today, it is time to give up the madness of our egos for the peace of God. It is time to become a child of God once more, and let ourselves be loved, because that is the truth, whether we realise it or not. It is time to give up the pushing, pulling, taking, weakness or domination of the ego, and let ourselves be loved, healed, guided and gifted, and embraced with tenderness and grace. The madness of separation leads to death, war, illness, fighting, hatred, fear, guilt, and all matter of negativity. Forgive God today and you will be forgiven for the attack and hidden guilt you projected onto God, making the most loving force in the universe seem angry and judgmental. This will allow gifts, grace and guidance back in. Today put yourself in God's hands or in the hands of your higher mind, a new day is about to dawn.

WAY 50 Happiness and Destiny

Just as you can tell how much a person is living their purpose by their level of fulfilment, you can also assess how well they have fulfilled their destiny by how happy they are.

Your purpose is something you do. Your destiny is something you are. If we all lived our destiny, we would have heaven on earth. As it is, most of us do not know or have not even thought about our destinies or our identities, except in a very limited context. The more of our destinies that we embrace, the more ego schemes we give up by letting go of things we thought would make us happy. This allows happiness in the here and now. When we think things will make us happy, those things possess us. When we think anything, anyone or any situation is the source of our happiness, we obsess about them, stop our flow and make ourselves dependent and needy. Our happiness comes from the extent of our relatedness and how much we give ourselves. An attachment shows a place where we are trying to take and this will lead to our defeat, hurt and heartbreak.

Letting go is crucial to happiness, for when we hold on, we are prevented from becoming who we 'came to be'. It keeps us from our potential, from reaching towards the future, and towards success.

If we do not reach that potential, we will never have the grace and happiness that can be shared with our partners and with the rest of the world.

Our destiny is tied in with our humanity and our divinity. It is knowing ourselves as God knows us, as his child. By embracing this self, by being who we have come to be, we ignite a certain light in the world that remains after we are gone. We give a certain gift to the world, to life, and to those around us, which blesses, heals and creates happiness. We become a lighthouse for humankind and a living treasure for the world. Our destiny opens up wisdom, knowledge and high levels of awareness.

By embracing our destinies, we become centred in our lives and so we set up a resonance that draws other people to their centres, where they find peace, innocence and grace. By embracing our destinies, we radiate love, and an openness to guidance and grace.

There is happiness here and now because there is no place to go and nothing to do to be happy. We need only receive it as grace and God's love for us. In terms of our destinies, we are no longer driven by the many goals and thought systems of the ego, so our minds become empty of thought, filled only with awareness, love, happiness and humour. The more we become empty of goal-directed thoughts, the more we feel the realisation of oneness. We become loving, happy and God-centred. We have learned to step back, relax, and let heaven lead the way. If there is anything to do, we will be guided to do it; if we are inspired to do something, we allow it to be done through us by grace. As our thinking and memory fall away, our awareness, humour, inspiration and intuition grow. As questions arise, the answers come in response from within us. As our needs, goals and acquisitiveness disappear, so does the future, replaced by the eternal now. As our ego recedes, there is less of us and more love, wisdom and light. We recognise the power of our minds to choose, and we direct the dream of our lives to a happy dream. More and more we opt for love and happiness. We have become truly effective.

We realise the power of our minds, and we understand that reality is much more fluid and flexible than we first thought. Yet, we do not carry the heavy burden of responsibility, but a response-ability. We listen more to our higher mind, realising that only it can free us and show us the way gracefully. We realise that everything happens for the best and that everything is evolving in the highest possible way, given what needs to be healed within us. We have become a master to the world, but nobody special to ourselves. The giving up of specialness allows for love to flow from heaven through us to others and the world and back again.

As masters, our love for others leads us to burn illusion and karma in the furnace of our hearts through love and compassion, saving others from disappointment, pain, self-imprisonment and self-repeating mistakes. We begin to challenge the very beliefs that claim and hazard humanity, such as illness, suffering, victimisation, scarcity (see page 195) and death, knowing them as only beliefs that can be transcended. At this point, we have gone beyond the polarisation of us and them, subject and object, and discovered instead a sense of we, an interconnectedness that seems evident at this level. We realise the unity of all things.

Here, there is only a desire for peace and a quiet mind, so that the splendours of heaven might rain down upon us and through us to humanity. Here, there is only joining, which heals the disturbances that arise, and the joy that comes of giving and receiving in love, especially God's love. Here we have let go of our pursuit of pleasure-pain or pain-pleasure and, paradoxically, delight and fulfilment lavish us as we seek to bless the world with healing balm and heaven's light. We live the life of a mystic, full of the Beloved's beauty and grace, and being a friend to the world, because we have embraced the Friend. Heaven comes nearer the earth, and the disheartened, weary and independent find the truth of love and partnership.

Exercise

Today, even letting go is not your job. Today is a day to embrace your destiny. Want your true identity as a beloved child of God, deserving every good thing. This spiritual legacy carries with it the common occurrence of miracles. Make a choice to give yourself fully to your destiny. Decide to go with it. You have a choice. Allowing this much of heaven to fill you will create an overflow that blesses the world in a continuous way.

Glossary

Bonding The connection that exists between us and others. Bonding creates love and success with ease rather than with struggle and difficulty. It is what gives cohesiveness its glue and teamwork its mutuality.

Compensation Compensation is an attempt to make up for something negative by acting in an opposite way, in a role-like fashion.

Conspiracy A chronic trap of the ego, set up so well that it looks like we will never escape it. Conspiracies are particularly difficult to heal until we realise that the problem has been set up that way.

Ego The part of us that seeks separation and special-ness and – ultimately – wants to be God. It is the part of us that fights for itself and its own needs first. It is built on fear, guilt, negativity, and competition, wanting to be the best of something, even if it is painful, or the best of the worst. Ego distracts, delays, and attempts to stop evolution, being more concerned with its own continuity. It is based on domination-subjugation, rather than any form of strength or truth. It is ultimately an illusion. We make it strong, while we are young, and then melt it away for partnership and grace.

Fusion A muddling of boundaries that occurs when bonding is lost. We cannot tell where we end and another begins. Fusion is the ego's answer to the lost intimacy. It is counterfeit bonding, which creates sacrifice and builds resentment. Fusion sets up an overburdening sense of loyalty. This eventually causes us to burn out and move into the opposite extreme of independence. We move from over-caring and smothering to acting as if we do not care.

Gifts Aspects of greatness or grace that make any job easy. Our gifts are the answer to all situations because they remove the problem. Gifts are learned lessons that continuously give and create flow. They are packets of wisdom, healing and responsiveness for the situation at hand. In every problem, there is a potential gift. We have thousands of unopened gifts within us that are the antidote to pain and problems.

Higher Mind The aspect of the mind that is creative, contains or receives all of our answers, opens our will and our spirit to the grace that heaven and the world around us wants to bestow on us. It is always guiding us with a quiet voice toward the truth. It encourages us to win together, not only now, but in the future.

Love This is the ultimate goal and the best means to the goal. It is the sweet fulfilment that comes of an open-hearted extension of oneself. This is the giving, receiving, sharing and reaching out to one another.

Love is the foundation of being and the best description of God, whatever your religious beliefs. It gives us everything we want – meaning, happiness, healing, nurturing, and joy. Our evolution and happiness are based on how much we give and receive in love.

Manifest To consciously use the mind to choose what we want. It is the use of visualisation, feeling and sensing what we want, and then letting it go and trusting. It allows us to create exactly what we want in detail.

Sacrifice A role that we take on to defend against a loss. When we are in sacrifice we give, but we do not receive, looking to lose now in the hope of winning later. Sacrifice is ineffective, blocking intimacy in an attempt to have the safety of a defence rather than equality and closeness.

Scarcity A fear-based belief that there is not enough and that we, or someone else, will have to go without. A belief in scarcity sets up power struggle, competition and sacrifice.

Shadow Figures Self-concepts that we have judged about ourselves and as a result, repressed. They represent areas of self-hatred that we project out onto others around us or onto the world in general.

Tantrum A choice in which we react, complain, withdraw or hurt ourselves when life does not come about as we consciously want. It can show itself as any form of failure, immaturity, or lack of success.

The stages of relationships All relationships go

through stages on their way to making heaven on earth. Each stage has its own challenges, traps and answers. If you know the stages of relationship, you are better prepared to handle the challenges and not to be blind-sided by the issues.

1.   Relationships begin in the Romance or Honeymoon Stage, where we idealise the other, yet it is in this stage that we can see and feel the potential of the relationship.

2.   Then there is the Power Struggle Stage where we are learning to bridge our differences, communicate, join and integrate both positions. Here we project out our shadow figures on our partner, and primarily fight for our needs.

3.   The Dead Zone is a stage where we are learning to transcend good form for authenticity, find our worth without roles or sacrifice and learn how to bond, moving beyond the counterfeit bonding of fusion.

4.   The Partnership Stage is where we have reached a balance between our own masculine-feminine sides and, correspondingly, we do so in our relationship with our partner, finding balance, equality and intimacy.

5.   The Leadership Stage is where we have both become leaders in life and have learned to value each other beyond the conflict and competition of personalities.

6.   The Vision Stage occurs when we have become a visionary along with our partner, making contributions to the earth and healing unconscious pain and fractures.

7. The Mastery Stage of relationships is where we have healed our feelings of failure and value-lessness to the point of moving from doing and becoming, to being and grace. This is where we become living treasures to the earth. It is the beginning of heaven on earth for our relationship.

Further Information

About the Psychology of Vision

PSYCHOLOGY
VISION of ®

For details on other books, the full range of audio and videotapes, and world-wide seminars, please contact us at:

Psychology of Vision UK
France Farm
Rushall
Pewsey
Wiltshire SN9 6DR
UK
Tel: +44 (0)1980 635199
e-mail: promotions@psychologyofvision.com
website: www.psychologyofvision.com

Also by Chuck Spezzano
(and available from the Psychology of Vision):
The Enlightenment Pack
Awaken the Gods